NEPTU

AND THE

POLLYWOGS

DOCUMENTING THE ROYAL NAVY'S
TRADITIONAL
CROSSING THE LINE CEREMONY

This book is researched, compiled and authored by

Paul White

in conjunction with the Royal Navy Research Archives.

This document records Royal Naval tradition and military social history.

http://www.royalnavyresearcharchive.org.uk/

DEDICATION

TOO ALL MY OLD OPPO'S

"We were all pollywogs once; you, me and the old hands.

He who has passed the bar and those still on patrol, in far off lands."

Paul White, Author

EPIGRAPH

"A sailor is not defined as much by how many seas he has sailed than by how many storms he has overcome."

Matshona Dhliwayo

FOREWORD

As the editor of the Royal Navy Research Archive, I have often encountered images and mentions of ships 'crossing the line' and the strange ceremony which is performed when the equator is crossed.

It is almost pantomime in its performance; it involves a host of elaboratively costumed characters following well-established scripts that have been handed down from mariner to mariner through the ages. The large cast enacts a series of events that involve some peculiar characters and rituals to initiate those who have not crossed the equator before, known as Pollywogs, by presenting them to King Neptune and his entourage.

On completion of some ordeals to prove their worthiness the initiates receive an often-ornate certificate conferring the Order of the Shellback.

To a lesser degree, there are also ceremonies and certificates for crossing the Arctic and Antarctic circles; Order of the Blue Nose and Order of the Red Nose.

The observance of these ceremonies has become so deeply entrenched in Royal Naval tradition it is performed in some form even in wartime.

So, what is behind these rituals and what are the experiences of those who have been through it?

I approached Paul with these questions in mind as the topic for a future book. I am well acquainted with his work having reviewed his four naval publications for the Royal Navy Research Archives website and felt this would be a good fit.

While I have access to historical materials, mostly from the Second World War, Paul has his own network of sources which can provide more contemporary and possibly contrasting, accounts of these rituals.

Tony Drury
Editor
The Royal Naval Research Archive

http://www.royalnavyresearcharchive.org.uk

TABLE OF CONTENT

Introduction — Page 1

History — Page 5

The Admiralty Pamphlet — Page 21

Parts and Characters — Page 49

Evolution — Page 63

Photographic plates — Pages 77

Evolution continued — Pages 86

HMS Deer Sound — Page 131

HME Perseus — Page 143

SS (RMS) Warrimoo — Page 153

Acknowledgements — Page 159

About the author — Page 160

Other books — Page 162

INTRODUCTION

THE LINE

*The **LINE** referred to in this book is the Earth's equator.*

The equator is an imaginary line of latitude around the Earths circumference, halfway between the North Pole and the South Pole, where the surface of the planet is parallel to the axis of rotation. This equatorial line divides the surface of the Earth into the northern and southern hemispheres.

The latitude of the Earth's equator is, by definition, 0° of arc.

The Earths equator is approximately 40,075 kilometres, that's 24,901 miles, in length, of which 78.8% lies across water and 21.3% over land. At the equator, day and night are of equal length all the year.

The name is derived from the medieval Latin 'aequator', used in the phrase 'circulus aequator diei et noctis',

meaning 'circle equalising day and night', itself from the Latin 'aequare' meaning to 'make equal'.

The Equator is one of the five notable circles of latitude on Earth. The other four are the Arctic Circle, 66°N; the Antarctic Circle, 66°S; the Tropic of Cancer, 23° N and the Tropic of Capricorn, 23°S.

The Equator is the only line of latitude which is a great circle, that is, one whose plane passes through the centre of the globe. The plane of Earth's equator, when projected outwards to the celestial sphere, defines the celestial equator.

INITIATION RITES

A traditional ceremony is frequently performed when one of H.M ships 'crosses the line'.

In its most simplistic form, the modern Crossing the Line ceremony is an initiation ritual, originally created by seasoned sailors to ensure their new shipmates were capable of handling long, rough times at sea.

The ceremony plays an integral role in fostering a sense of identity, camaraderie and brotherhood among ships companies, by initiating novices or 'pollywogs', the sailors who have not yet crossed the equator, into 'the Ancient Order of the Deep.'

On the day of the crossing, a procession, with 'Father Neptune' and his 'royal court' takes place. Members of the royal court coerce the 'pollywogs' to complete a series of uncomfortable tasks until they are finally submerged into tanks of water, eventually, to emerge as fully-fledged Matelots and receive certificates of confirmation.

Records from the early 19th century report the ceremony could be a brutal affair, sometimes involving sailors to be beaten with boards and wet ropes before being thrown or 'dunked' overboard. During these times, the Crossing the Line ceremony was more a test of physical endurance and perseverance against pain than the high jinks carried out in today's initiation rites.

Nowadays, Crossing the Line is intended to be fun, albeit still with a little of the rough and tumble from earlier years. The ceremony is created and executed using wit, wisdom, and reference to classical literature[*1] and high theatre.

The ceremony involves elaborate costuming, props and stage effects. Each is planned as a stage production with the individual crossing scripts carefully written and rehearsed in secret.

It is often said the Crossing the Line ceremony is a seafaring tradition dating back to the middle-ages.

However, the ceremony has its roots in much earlier times.

ELUCIDATING NOTE.

Initiation is a rite of passage marking entrance or acceptance into a group or society. It can also be a formal admission to adulthood in a community or one of its formal components. In an extended sense,

---

[1] Although rarely accurately.

it can also signify a transformation in which the initiate is 'reborn' into a new role.

Examples of initiation ceremonies might include Hindu Diksha, Christian baptism or confirmation, Jewish bar or bat mitzvah, acceptance into a fraternal organization, secret society or religious order, or graduation from school or recruit training. A person taking the initiation ceremony in traditional rites is called an initiate

Psychological

In the study of certain social forms of initiation, laboratory experiments in psychology suggest severe initiations produce cognitive dissonance. Dissonance is then thought to produce feelings of strong group attraction among initiates after the experience because they want to justify the effort used.

Rewards during initiations have important consequences in that initiates who feel more rewarded express stronger group identity. As well as group attraction, initiations can also produce conformity among new members. Psychology experiments have also shown initiations increase feelings of affiliation.

In addition, there are similar rites of passages associated with parts of naval and military life, which do not constitute true initiations as the participants are already and remain members of the same community.

One such rite is associated with crossing the equator on board a naval ship.

HISTORY

THEORY AND GENESIS

Since nautical history began, seafaring folk held some form of ceremony when they passed a certain point of their voyage. That point could be when passing a certain headland or after rounding a particular cape. These ceremonies may have been to thank their Gods for safe passage or to boost the morale of novice sailors. It is recorded the Vikings, Phoenicians and Dutch all held a form of voyage thanksgiving.

For the modern Sailor, these traditional customs are generally limited to the 'Crossing the Line' ceremonies. There are five 'lines' commonly associated with various rites of passage, they are the are the Arctic Circle, the Tropic of Cancer, the Equator, the Tropic of Capricorn and the Antarctic Circle.

This book exclusively focuses on the ceremonial activities performed by the ship's companies of the Royal Navy when crossing the Equator. Which is typically marked by a ritual involving Neptune the god of the seas, a ceremony loosely related to that of the ancient Athenians.

When Greek civilization was in its prime, way before Romulus and Remus were even twinkle in their father's eyes, there was Poseidon. History recalls, 'His domain was of Hercules and he had some authority'. He was the god of the seas to whom the ancient matelots burned incense and sang his praises.

Poseidon, who would whip-up the odd storm, throw a crash of thunder and a few bursts of lightning into the mix, just to scare the living daylights out of those poor ancient Greek sailors, was doing rather well for himself. In fact, he had done so for several hundred years and was living happily ever after... Until those pesky Romans turned up.

After a lot of argy-bargy the Romans eventually beat the Greeks and took over the seas. However, the god Poseidon continued to make a fair old bit of roughers, which pissed the Romans off no-end.

The Romans answer was to obtain the services of one of their own gods, one who could stuff it to old Poseidon and, in effect, put the old giffer out of business.

The problem was, the Romans did not have a spare god hanging around Olympus at the time, they were all far too busy killing humans, eating, drinking and fornicating; so the canny Roman sods borrowed a god from the Etruscans. *(They never returned him either.)*

This god's name was Nethuns or Nethunus, depending on which part of Etruscia you came from. But what was a little miss pronunciation to a Roman? So, instead of getting all tongue-tied, the Romans called him Neptunus.

This left poor old Poseidon in deep do dos and needing his welly boots.

Now, this is where it gets complicated but very interesting, so grab a tot and pull up a bollard...

Poseidon was chatting up some bird called Amphitrite. She was the daughter of Oceanus, himself a very big cheese in the Greeks system of gods and all that stuff. Oceanus was the primordial Titan god of the great, earth-encircling River Okeanos, the font of all the earth's fresh water, rivers, wells, springs, rain clouds and so on.

Anyway... Poseidon had gone to some amazing lengths to trap this Amphitrite woman, *(supposedly still a virgin at the time, but this is challenged, so who knows the truth?)* Many of those lengths Poseidon took to attract Amphitrite did not particularly please the ungrateful bitch, so she legged it, running off to a place called Mount Atlas.

When Poseidon heard about his girlfriend absconding, he got a bit miffed and sent one of his dolphin gods, 'Delphines', to convince her he was really husband material; but by the time the dolphin found Amphitrite she had been adopted by a new bloke who had recently moved into the neighbourhood. He was called Neptunus and this adoption now made him Poseidon's father-in-law. *(sort of, but this is ancient Rome/Greek, so it's all twisted anyway.)*

Obviously, old Poseidon was gutted by this news, but he married the ungrateful bitch anyway.

Not that he remained faithful for more than the first five minutes of their relationship, preferring to get jiggy with just about anyone, anything and everything that moved.

Eventually, though, old Poseidon got so pissed off with Neptune stealing his position as God of the seas he ended up committing suicide by drowning himself in his own ocean.

Now, skipping on a bit in time and getting back to the ceremony, it seems not many people wrote about it for ages and I mean 'ages', as in a distinct period of history.

It is not until we read accounts from recent history, accounts referred to as 'modern day' although they are still quite old, do we see any accounts of crossing the line recorded for posterity. *(One of the reasons for this book.)*

In fact, our present-day scholars say the true origins are *'shrouded in mystery'* and they can only *'guess at the dates of inception as somewhere between 1768 and 1818'*... and then we find an account from a French ship in the early sixteenth century, (1529 to be exact), where the journal of the French sailor, Robert Durand describes the ceremony as:

"A baptism of the tropics – a carnivalesque inversion of the religious order and social hierarchy – designed to create solidarity among ordinary crew members."

A discovery which stuffs the venerated, but biased, Professor Callender's opinion, who reckoned the custom was brought into being in the Royal Navy's East Indian Command during Nelson's day. (*Nelson died in October 1805*).

Callender's statement was based on the general thinking of the era that all things naval originated during Nelson's time. It was an easy statement to make, but one which was proven to be as absurd and as stupid as he.

Nevertheless, unproven history is rife with such assumption and opinion.

If one looks further back in time, they can speculate the roots of the seagoing ceremony may be traced to the Phoenicians and even the Vikings.

Here is a brief insight into those claims.

THE VIKING THEORY

Our modern practice is believed to have evolved from Viking rituals, executed upon crossing the 30th parallel, a tradition passed on to the Anglo-Saxons and Normans in Britain according to A.B. Campbell (RN).[2]

ÆGIR (Aegir)

Manhood was not something given in the Viking Age, a boy had to earn it. Viking men were expected to provide for and protect his family.

According to old Scandinavian law books, a boy was generally considered a man after 15 winters had passed. In Iceland, it was "hestefør og drikkefør", meaning once he was able to ride a horse and was accepted as a drinking partner by the other men.

Aegir is the god of the sea in Norse mythology.

---

[2] A.B. Campbell, Customs and Traditions of the Royal Navy. Aldershot: Gale & Polden Limited, 1956

His wife, the sea goddess, Ran, with whom he has nine daughters, the billow maidens, who were believed to move the waves.

Aegir was both worshipped and feared by sailors, they believed Aegir and his wife, Ran would use nets to capture sailors before taking them down into his underwater kingdom. Captain's would give coins to every sailor, so if they were captured, they would have a gift for the gods.

Sacrifices were made to appease him, particularly prisoners before setting sail. Saxon pirates would often sacrifice every tenth prisoner, ensuring a safe journey across Aegir's sea. Aegir was shown as a powerful god, often holding a spear, an uncanny likeness to the Greek god Poseidon.

The Goddess Ran was also dangerous and extremely hostile. Using her fishing net, she would drag any sailor she caught into the deep dark ocean.

Because the Vikings feared Ran, they would offer tribute to her before embarking on raids, in the hope of a safe return.

> *And Sigrun above, brave in battle,*
>
> *protected them and their vessel;*

the king's sea-beasts twisted powerfully,

out of Ran's hand toward Gnipalund

'Ogress, you stood before the prince's ships

and blocked the fjord mouth;

the king's men you were going to give to Ran,

if a spear hadn't lodged in your flesh

THE PHOENICIAN CONNECTION

The Phoenicians, for example, gave sacrifices to their sea god upon passing the 'Pillars of Hercules', *today's Straits of Gibraltar.*

Yamm

In versions of the Phoenician myth, Yamm, the chaotic force, is in constant conflict with Baal, the force of order. Baal and Yamm meet in combat on the plains of heaven. Yamm is defeated and cast out, into the chaos of the sea.

Even so, Yamm wants to dethrone Baal and rule heaven and so he returns from the depths of the sea to battle for heaven's gates, bringing chaos again, in a never-ending cycle.

Each time, Yamm is exiled to the seas he directs his rage against humans. Yamm and Baal continually kill each other, resurrect, fight and die, only to return to life once more.

Yamm has been associated with the Greek god Poseidon in his more violent and spiteful moments. Yamm is taken from the Semitic word for 'sea', also known as Yam.

Yam-Nahar was the god of the sea in the pantheon of the Canaanite-Phoenicians. Depicted consistently as tyrannical, angry, violent and harsh. Yamm was the brother of Mot, the god of death, associated with chaos, an association with Lotan the Leviathan, the monster who churned the seas.

OVERVIEW

Ancient seafarers had no percept of modern man-made lines drawn around the earth, so could not associate with such ambiguous conception. Instead, they performed rituals and ceremonies based on a combination of cultural beliefs and the knowledge of the waters on which they sailed.

As one could expect, there are countless accounts of rituals before a ship sailed and so, when safely docked in harbour after a voyage.

But there are also numerous accounts, from many civilisations, of rites and rituals undertaken when passing certain headlands, through narrow straits, or dangerous waters, such as a gulf or delta.

Many ancients created or adopted gods and goddesses, many whom had special places aboard their ships, often on the stern or at the bow. Some vessels were named after these deities as a way of asking for divine protection and safe passage.

Today's superstitions particular to sailors and mariners, most which are common around the world, are based in the inherent risks of sailing and luck, either good or bad, as well as portents and omens. Many of these come from traditional nautical stories, folklore, tropes, myths and legend believed as fact by these ancient seafarers.

To end this section...

The expansion of trade routes in the early sixteenth century and funding for exploration required European vessels to regularly cross the equator.

The equator, marked as '0' degrees latitude, is a conceptualised dividing line between the north and south hemispheres, which set the stage for the development of a rite of passage.

The early equatorial rituals were primarily comprised of a religious ceremony, a thanksgiving for having passed this point of the passage and a baptism, symbolising the ships passing from one 'world', the old, to the 'next', the new.

By the mid-sixteenth century, sailors began to regard 'Crossing the Line' as a right to baptise those who had not crossed the equator previously.

This initiation ceremony soon spread to other European ships and, as it did, became more complex in its form, as sailing during that age necessitated the ability to depend and rely on one's shipmates. The ritual, therefore, developed to become an initiation of inexperienced members of a ship's company.

These inexperienced hands were literally and figuratively put 'on trial'.

Literally during the ceremony with its mock trial.

Figuratively because the ritual tested the strength of character of the sailors.

In outline, the unproven members of the ship's company put themselves into the hands of more experienced seamen who performed numerous invasive 'operations' to heal and clean, until the sailors are back to a 'new-born' state, often shaven and covered in blood.

After which they are baptised and, often, given a new name. *(One of the reasons why nicknames are so entrenched in Royal Naval culture to this day.)*[3]

Thus, the ritual produced a man who had stood trial, passed the tests. Emerging as a new man, now accepted as one of the brotherhood of a ship's company.

Petty Officer John Bechervaise commented on Crossing the Line when aboard **HMS Blossom** 1825. He said the inexperienced,

"were to be initiated into the mysteries of crossing the Equinoctial line and entering the dominions of Neptune".

This wording invokes the 'mysteries' imparted by the guilds and trade societies of the time, even Masonic lodges of that generation.

---

[3] 'The Andrew, Jack & Jenny, Royal Navy nicknames – origin & history' by Paul White. Toad Publishing ISBN-13: 978-1723841149

In this interpretation, King Neptune takes the role of patron for which Christian saints had for the different trades on land: St Crispin for shoemakers, St Clement for blacksmiths and Bishop Blaize for wool-combers are all documented examples.

The ship was also a floating world of work, a self-contained society where all lived and worked. The messes, in some respect, compared with pre-industrial households.

A ship, however, was a highly specialised workplace, with most sailors having particular skills which, when brought together in harmony, produced an efficient, well-oiled and happy environment.

On long journeys, the ship's company lived together in cramped, relatively unpleasant conditions and the crew's morale was a major matter for the commanding officers.

The Crossing the Line ceremony was one means whereby a sense of solidarity could be reinforced, bringing everyone together, including midshipmen and officers, into a select society under the authority of King Neptune.

At times a certain robustness could spill over into violence, usually in defence of what were assumed to be 'traditional rights'.

These were usually referencing long-standing local customs or practices such as an allowance to play 'rough music'[*4] and skimmingtons[*5]. Elements of this plebeian moral economy can be witnessed in the crossing the line ceremony, it gave the crew the opportunity of taking some revenge on the unpopular men, especially those who were deemed to have violated maritime norms or customs.

When this involved meting out harsh treatment to their superiors, an element of inversion and misrule became apparent, in which lower-deck grievances were redressed in a customary and, therefore legitimate, controlled manner.

The miserly purser on Bechervaise's ship, for example, was forced to surrender two bottles of rum and some porter before he was released, a larger gift than was expected from his fellow officers.

John Cunningham, surgeon on the Cambridge in 1824, only discovered his assistant was unpopular with the crew when he was treated very roughly when crossing the line.

---

[4] Rough Music, a loud cacophony created with tin pans, drums, etc.

[5] Skimmingtons, loud singing and chanting. Originating from masked processions outside the home of a wrongdoer, involving the cacophonous rattling of bones cleavers, bells, hooting, bull's horns, banging of frying pans, saucepans, kettles, or other kitchen or barn implements with the intention of creating long-lasting embarrassment to the alleged perpetrator

The foundations of the nautical ceremony can be traced from these vague academic accounts, though the ancient chronicles and historical journals to modern day reports.

However, with the introduction of modern electronic devices, such as tablets, phones and digital cameras. Written descriptions of the current ceremony are once again dwindling, much as they did during the second world war, albeit for very different reasons.

With the recent major ground shift in social acceptance creating 'Snowflake'*6 generations, the longevity of this ancient and traditional ritual may soon disappear from the Royal Navy altogether, or at least morph into some unrecognisable facsimile, where jovial offence and minor physical contact are forbidden altogether.

That would be a sad day.

---

6 Snowflake, a neologistic term used to characterise those prone to taking offense and less resilient than previous generations. Being too emotionally vulnerable to cope with views that challenge their own.

THE ADMIRALTY PAMPHLET

In **September 1946,** the British Admiralty issued a pamphlet entitled;

Crossing the Line:

'An account of the origins of the ceremonies traditionally connected with Crossing the Line, together with a Procedure for the conduct of those ceremonies and examples of the Documents associated therewith.'

Thanks to the Records of the Admiralty in the National Archives, I am able to give a summary of the text of the pamphlet.

The Foreword runs thus:

It is not the intention to lay down a hard and fast drill for Crossing the Line. To do so would not only be an impertinence but would ignore such factors as the size of the ship, the local talent available, and the general circumstances prevailing at the time.

With the return to peace routine, however, and the obvious necessity to foster an awareness of the old traditions in the minds of the rising generation, many requests have been received for the promulgation of an authentic order of proceedings.

This pamphlet has therefore been produced on the clear understanding that it represents no more than a symposium of the basic features involved, and in the hope that it may be of practical assistance to those who wish to observe the appropriate ceremonies with the dignity and regard for accuracy to which they are by custom and tradition entitled.

In compiling these notes, considerable reference has been made to 'Crossing the Line in **H.M.S. Renown**,'[*] and acknowledgement are also due to Frank C. Bowen, Esq., Commander R. T. Gould, R. N. (Retd.), and to various officers for their assistance.

Part I,

Origins of the ceremony

The ceremonies connected with Crossing the Line are pagan in origin.

In their earlier forms, they were not even associated with the Equator but were in the nature of sacrifices to propitiate the gods when entering the unknown.

Straits and narrow passages, in addition to representing a transition to hitherto unexplored waters, held very real terrors for seamen on account of the purely physical hazards presented by strong and unpredictable currents, sudden gusts of winds, rocks and shoals.

Early records show that some sort of ceremony was connected with areas such as the Straits of Gibraltar, the Sound and the Skaw.

Forfeit was paid by the ship rather than by the individual, and there is a suggestion of human sacrifice in the early Viking days. The theory has, in fact, been advanced that the ducking of initiates, now the main feature of the present ceremonies, is derived from the actual throwing of a human body into the sea in moments of peril.

Chaplain Teonge, 1675, refers in his diary to the ducking from the yardarm of men entering the Straits of Gibraltar for the first time, or being required to pay one dollar in lieu.

By the old laws, the mariner did not remove his clothes from beginning to end of voyage, and Captain Woodes Rogers, referring to the customary ducking "when entering the Tropic," adds that this was of great benefit in enabling many "to recover the colour of their skins which were grown very black and nasty."

This may be symbolised in the lathering and shaving of novices which is now part of the proceedings, but there is no sort of supporting evidence to this effect.

It seems more probable the lathering and other ministrations have grown up as part of the mummery associated with any form of initiation.

In any case, it is clear that much of the traditional ceremony is indistinguishable from the universal custom of "blooding" initiates, and so the final result is probably a combination of this custom and the symbolic remains of the original propitiatory offerings to the sea-god.

In the course of time, both the Equator and the Arctic Circle became the scene of traditional ceremonies, as marking the limits of fresh enterprise, and to those who had not previously crossed them the boundaries of the "unknown."

The custom of paying forfeits, either in money or in kind, in order to avoid the rigours of initiation, no longer obtains.

Part II

Dramatis Personae

King Neptune

Doctor

Barber

Barber's Assistant(s)

Queen Amphitrite

King's Messenger

Herald(s)

Trumpeter(s)

Judge

Judge's Clerk

Policemen

Head Bear(s)

Bodyguard Bears

Notes;

(i) The above characters are not all essential. On the other hand, certain additions are permissible, e.g. Mermaids, Ladies-in-Waiting, etc.

(ii) In a big ship, it is sometimes the practice for the principal parts to be taken by Officers or Warrant Officers. When V.I.P.s are to take part in the Ceremonies, this is considered to be essential, a special team of Officer Bears being enrolled to initiate them.

Part III

The Preliminary Function

The main ceremony of initiation, by its very nature, must rightly and inevitably involve an element of horseplay, but the preliminaries can and should be so handled as to make a lasting impression on those who witness them for the first time.

These preliminaries, which represent the approach of the ship to King Neptune's domain, take place after supper on the evening of the day before that on which the ship crosses the Line. The Daily Orders for that day should contain an item in the following sense:—

The ship, being within hailing distance of the Equator, will probably be boarded by an Emissary from the Court of King Neptune. On sighting this Emissary, the hands will be piped forward to witness his arrival.

The setting for the Herald's arrival must, of course, depend on the size of the ship and the resources available.

The following treatment is suited to a cruiser or above.

Preparations

Run two or more old wash-deck hoses across the upper deck just forward of the breakwater and connect to mains.

Hoses should have small holes pierced in them of the right size and number to produce a vertical curtain of water about 6 or 8 feet high when the mains are fully opened.

Rig green floodlights, yardarm groups, or "footlights" to illuminate the water curtain, all lights being on a dimmer circuit. Rig spotlights to illuminate figures standing in the eyes of the ship.

If available, rig loudspeakers to sound aft from the forecastle, with the microphone concealed in a conch-shell or on the Herald's staff.

Drill

Pipe: *"D'ye hear there? The ship is expected to be within hailing distance of the Equator in ten minute's time."*

When spectators are mustered (all abaft the breakwater), bring up water curtain and floodlights slowly. Under cover of water curtain the following muster as quickly as possible in the eyes of the ship:

Trumpeters Herald Bears.

Fanfare on trumpets, followed by a throaty roar of laughter through the loudspeakers.

Herald: *"Ahoy — What ship?"*

Captain (from the bridge): *"Her Britannic Majesty's Ship . . ."*

Herald: *"Who commands this ship?"*

Captain: *"Captain ... Royal Navy"* (adding decorations in full, e.g.

Companion of the Distinguished Service Order, etc.)

Herald: *"Stop the ship — I wish to come onboard."* (Ring down Stop Both)

Captain: *"The way is off my ship."*

(Lower water curtain, bring up spotlights on Herald and attendants)

Herald: *"Whence come you, and whither bound?"*

Captain: *"We come from . . . and we are bound for . . . We crave permission to clear the Line and proceed southward."*

It is sometimes the custom for the Captain to descend to the forecastle at this point.)

Herald: *"My Royal Master, being advised of your approach, bids me welcome you and those who sail with you. That all things may be done properly and in due order, he makes known his wishes by Proclamation, duly signed, and to which attend ye all."*

(Unrolls Proclamation. Fanfare of trumpets. Bears growl and assume belligerent attitudes.)

"Whereas it has pleased us to convene a Court to be held onboard Her Britannic Majesty's Ship ... on the upper deck thereof at. . . on . . . the said Ship being then on the Equator in Longitude . . .

"By these presents we summon all those who have not heretofore entered our Domains to tender the usual homage and to be initiated into the mystic rites according to the ancient usages of our Kingdom. Whereof nor you nor any of you may fail, as you will answer at your peril, and to the delight of our trusty Bodyguard." (Short fanfare on trumpets — Bears relax)

Captain: *"It shall be done. And now, ere you depart, will you take some refreshment?"*

(Captain's Steward serves beer to all. Some apprehension displayed by Bears, who are served last, as to their inclusion in the invitation. They should drink from bottles, the Herald and the Trumpeters from glasses.)

Herald: *"I now return whence I came. Pray cause these documents.to be served upon those of your Company who come newly to the domains of my Royal Master. Farewell until the morning."*

Captain: *"Farewell until the morning."*

(Herald hands heavily sealed package to Captain — Fanfare on trumpets, during which cut spotlights and bring up water curtain slowly. As curtain reaches full height and ship gathers way, repeat throaty laughter.)

Notes;

(i) It is held by some authorities that Neptune and his full Court should attend the preliminaries set out above, but this procedure is considered to be not only illogical but profoundly bad theatre.

(ii) There is no sort of reason, if space permits, why the Herald should not appear in a nautical chariot drawn by Dolphins, or other symbolic vehicles.

(iii) In an aircraft carrier, the advantages of using the forward lift for the arrival and departure of the Herald and his attendants will be obvious, and similar remarks apply to the main ceremony on the following day.

(iv) It is by no means essential to provide an individual Summons for each "initiate," but these documents are frequently treasured by the recipients just as much as the "Crossing the Line" Certificates.

The alternative is to broadcast the terms of the document and post copies on the Notice Boards. Individual Summonses, if issued, should follow the lines of the Herald's Proclamation set out above, the name of the individual being shown on a separate line in substitution for the words: "All those who have not heretofore entered our Domains."

The main ceremony

Preparations Routine

The Ship's Routine should be so adjusted that nothing is done after scrubbing decks. The hands should be piped to breakfast as early as possible, and to clean into skylarking rig.

It is sometimes the practice to get out a completely bogus routine, embracing such items as "Bears to cocoa and wash." The advantage of this procedure is that it provides a useful programme of events and adds one more document for the record.

Rigging

The essential requirement is a stage, platform or dais, a canvas bath, and a chair or chairs capable of being tilted in such a manner that the occupant is precipitated backwards into the bath.

If the number of initiates is sufficient, two or more chairs may be provided, and possibly two baths, side by side. The baths should be placed with the longer side running away from the platform. The water should be about 4 feet deep, and it is well to place some suitable cushioning material under the baths to prevent injury in the event of any initiates receiving an extra heavy "bumping."

Arrangements should be made for the water to be changed at frequent intervals.

Properties

The second requirement is the "lather" for use by the Court Barbers. The essential point is lavish and simple application, and somewhat staggering quantities may be required. The normal recipe calls for a paste of flour and water in white and two other colours, but in these days of food rationing, some less palatable substitute may have to be found.

The remaining properties, in the construction of which much ingenuity may be displayed, i.e. as follows:—

Stethoscope (e.g. Voice-pipe headpiece)

Thermometer (e.g. Gauge glass)

Lancet (e.g. Cutlass or Javelin)

Medicine (Sea-water, with a flavouring of quinine, in a large variety of bottles)

Pills (Dough, "bound" if desired with horse-hair, and flavoured with garlic or other tasty but harmless concoction)

Razors (Made of carefully smoothed wood)

Shaving brushes (Whitewash brush size)

Note;

The common attribute of all these properties is their exaggerated size.

Costumes

In general, the design of the costumes can be left to local talent and imagination.

The Bears, however, not only have to look something like Bears, but they have to spend the greater part of the day in the bath.

There are many ways of meeting these requirements, but the following specification, taken from the account of H.M.S. Renown when Crossing the Line in April 1920, may be of help:

The basic part of the costume was black canvas lightly thrummed with yarns.

A fearsome embellishment of teased-out spun yarn, like phenomenal furs of an unknown species, thickly draped their necks, shoulders and waists ... on their heads, they wore navy socks in the manner of fishermen's caps.

The important point is that the "foundation" should be strong enough to withstand the clutching hands of struggling initiates.

Identification of Initiates

There are four methods by which those who have not previously crossed the Line can be identified:—

(a) By inspection of Service Certificates — laborious and not 100% certain.

(b) By direct enquiry — not very satisfactory and tends to detract from the excitement.

(c) By a detailed enquiry addressed to Leading Hands of Messes, calling for the names of those members of their Mess who have previously crossed the Line, and if more than twice, how many times — a laborious but satisfactory method, giving the names of initiates by elimination, and identifying those old hands who may be entitled to some special distinction by virtue of numerous crossings.

(d) By direct "hunting out" by the Policemen — traditionally, this is the correct method, but it is not easy in a big ship and tends to lose its interest and entertainment value if too prolonged.

It is, however, desirable that a few volunteer "reluctant participants" should be found to open the proceedings, as described later.

Procedure

It is customary for much of the main ceremony, and particularly the earlier stages thereof, to be conducted in verse. Once again, this must be arranged in the light of local circumstances and available talent, but it is worth noting that overmuch doggerel tends to become a weariness of the flesh.

The proceedings open with the assembly, in some suitable spot, of King Neptune and his Court. (Once again, it will be noted that the lift of an aircraft carrier provides an admirable piece of stage machinery.)

Preceded by the Music, Policemen and Bears, and followed by the remainder of their Entourage, King Neptune and Queen Amphitrite, seated in a nautical equipage drawn by Dolphins, then make a professional tour of the upper deck, finishing either on the Quarter-deck or at the Royal Dais, as deemed most convenient.

Here they are greeted by the Captain, and after a formal exchange of amenities, those persons qualified by previous multiple crossings of the Line are presented.

The ceremony is made the occasion for the investiture of these veterans with Orders and Certificates appropriate to their rank, service and personal idiosyncrasies, the necessary insignia being fabricated onboard.

This is a suitable stage in the proceedings to tackle the question of lady initiates.[*7]

There have been instances when Flag Officers or Captain's wives have been present, and the usual practice has been to grant them honorary certificates and to make them members of an appropriate Order.

For example, the Bev. A. Bloxam, Chaplain of **H.M.S. Blonde** (Captain Lord Byron) notes in his diary for 12th November 1824, that Queen Amphitrite "addressed a few lines to Lady B."

While on the occasion of **H.M.S. New Zealand** crossing the Line on 6th May 1919, it is recorded that "... At this stage, Her Majesty (Queen Amphitrite), with much graciousness and charm of manner conferred the insignia of the Most Unfathomable Order of the Deep Sea Needle, First Class, upon Lady Jellicoe."

---

[7] The ceremony has been adapted now female sailors serve aboard HM ships. The WRNS were finally integrated into the regular Royal Navy in 1993, although it was In October 1990, during the Gulf War, on HMS Brilliant when the first women to be 'officially recognised' served on an operational warship.

The account subsequently states that the distinguished novice was graciously excused homage, a few drops of sea-water being sprinkled on her head in token of full initiation.

When these formalities are completed, the whole procession moves to the scene of action, King Neptune and Queen Amphitrite take their seats, the Herald makes a short proclamation, the Doctor, Barbers, etc., report all present and correct, King Neptune orders: "Bears in the Bath," and the business of the day begins.

It is well to open with two or three volunteers, one of whom should be an officer, who will undertake to act as "reluctant initiates." Which is to say, they have to be sought out by the Policemen, they resist arrest, and, generally speaking, are put through the hoop.

The reading of bogus Punishment Warrants prior to the final administrations of the Barber, Doctor, etc., lends colour to this part of the proceedings and aggravates the apprehension of the remaining initiates.

Events then take their normal course, the drill being as follows;

(a) The initiate is produced by the Policemen or comes forward voluntarily.

(b) His name is announced, and a notation made against it in a massive tome by the Clerk.

(c) He is seated in the chair, his temperature is taken, heart tested, pulse timed, etc., etc.

(d) He is lathered and shaved, a pill is popped into his mouth, and he is tipped backwards into the bath, there to be dealt with by the Bears according to his deserts.

Certificates

It is worth taking a good deal of trouble over the layout of the Certificates, and in the selection of a firm to reproduce them in colour.

The essential features are;

(a) The ship's crest

(b) A photograph or drawing of the ship

(c) The main body of the Certificate

(d) The seals of Neptune and Amphitrite

With regard to (c) above, there is no hard and fast rule, and the following is merely taken from an actual Certificate by way of example:

Be it Hereby known that . . . has been duly initiated into the Ancient and Mystic rites of our Realm as by our Royal Decree from time Immemorial. Further ... We hereby require all such as have not yet entered our Domains, to treat the aforesaid with all respect to which our duly initiated and loyal subjects are entitled.

Given at our Court on board Her Britannic Majesty's Ship ... on the Equator in Longitude . . . This . . . Day of ... 19... (Seal)

If the ship is on a special cruise or particularly interesting foreign commission, a scroll showing the places visited adds to the ornamentation of the Certificate.

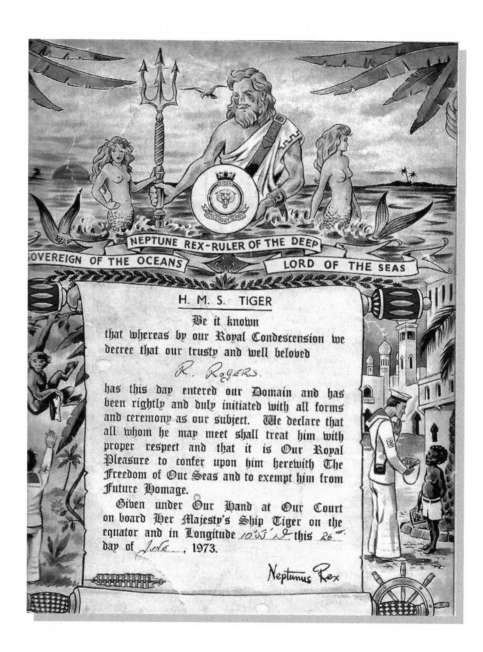

Author's Notes.

(1) The Admiralty pamphlet of 1946 basis its advice and suggestions from the Crossing the Line ceremony held aboard HMS Renown, a 15inch gun Battlecruiser, on Friday and Saturday 16th and 17th of April respectively, in 1920.

I find this of no surprise, as that particular crossing is possibly one of the most photographed, documented and detailed recordings of any equatorial crossing in history.

The reason being, HMS Renown was on 'Royal cruise' to Australia and New Zealand.

On board was HRH Edward, Prince of Wales, who was to become King Edward VIII. *(At least for a short while in 1936, until he abdicated due to his romance with Mrs, Wallis Simpson.)*

Clearly the Captain, Ernest A. Taylor, who commanded the Renown from 14th of January 1919 to the 2nd of August 1921, wished to ensure the ceremony was as organised and as practised as any West End theatre production.

This proved a defining moment in the evolution of the Royal Navy's staging of the Crossing the Line ceremony.

It has left a legacy of which has shaped all initiation rites and rituals performed by the Royal Navy's ships companies since.

The official recognition is reinforced in the 1946 admiralty pamphlet.

(2) 1990/93 was not the first-time women served onboard a British warship.

It is a persistent myth that war has always been an all-male affair and women in combat zones, whatever their activities, were 'civilians' and not 'warriors.' This becomes a confusing distinction in practice because men and women under fire often do the same things.

It is particularly confusing in the case of naval warfare, because at sea everyone aboard, male, female, gunner, carpenter or nurse is, quite literally, in the same boat.

When a ship is fired upon, everyone aboard is at war.

During the eighteenth century, large numbers of women followed their sailor husbands to sea. A few even joined their husbands on battleships. The British Admiralty officially did not 'officially' allow women on board, but records show captains often let the wives of officers join the ship and share their husbands' cabins, hammocks and daily ration of salted beef, dried peas, hardtack, and cheese.

Life was harsh back then and most women had no home or money while their husbands were at sea. The ship provided a home and a chance to share life, however tough, with their husbands. The wives worked on the ship, mending or cleaning clothes or serving as captains' maids. In battle, they attended the wounded or carried gunpowder.

Childbirth at sea was not uncommon, and sometimes a ship's guns were fired to hasten a difficult birth, a practice which gave rise to the saying, *'a son of a gun.'*

During the Napoleonic Wars, Captain W. N. Glascock of the Royal Navy wrote;

"This day the surgeon informed me that a woman on board had been labouring in childbirth for twelve hours if I could see my way to permit the firing of a broadside to leeward, nature would be assisted by the shock. I complied with the request and she was delivered a fine male child."

PARTS AND CHARACTERS

The list of characters itemised in the previous section is by no means comprehensive as ship to ship, year to year, ceremony to ceremony, the players and performers morph, evolve and alter to suit.

The following is a wider list of possible characters who may, or may not, be used or created for the crossing the line ceremony.

THE CEREMONIAL CHARACTERS

King Neptune

(See cover photo.)

Imperium Neptuni Regis translates to "The Empire of King Neptune."

Neptune was the god of freshwater and the sea in Roman religion. While he is generally considered to be the Roman counterpart of the

Greek god Poseidon this is wrong. They are two totally different gods.[8]

In the Greek-influenced tradition, Neptune was the brother of Jupiter and Pluto; the brothers presided over the realms of Heaven, the earthly world and the Underworld.

Neptune was also worshipped by the Romans as a god of horses, under the name Neptunus Equester.

Which also gives the link to the white tops of waves, often referred to as 'White Horses'.

---

[8] See Theory and Genesis, page 5 of this book.

Queen Amphitrite

AMPHITRITE, or in ancient Roman mythology, SALACIA, was the goddess-queen of the sea, wife of Poseidon and eldest of the fifty Nereides.

Nereids are sea nymphs, female spirits of sea waters, they are the 50 daughters of Nereus and Doris. They symbolise everything beautiful and kind about the sea. Their melodious voices sang as they danced around their father.

They are represented as very beautiful girls, crowned with branches of red coral and dressed in white silk robes trimmed with gold, but who went barefoot.

They are part of Poseidon's entourage and carry his trident. The Nereids can be friendly and helpful to sailors, like the Argonauts in their search for the Golden Fleece.

But when Poseidon first sought Amphitrite's hand in marriage, she fled his advances, hiding herself away near Atlas in the Ocean stream at the far ends of the earth. The dolphin-god Delphin eventually tracked her down and persuading Amphitrite to return and wed the sea-king, but not until after Neptune had adopted her making himself

Poseidon's father-in-law. A fact which led to Poseidon taking his own life.

Herald

The whole ceremony starts when the ship is 'hailed' by Neptune's herald.

Judge

Hands out the sentences to the Pollywogs.

Davy Jones

The origin of Davy Jones is unclear. As is when he became a prime character in this ceremony.

There have been numerous attempts find a definitive answer, with the most prominent tales appearing in movies and books, such as Disney's Pirates of the Caribbean which is loosely based on the story of the ghost ship 'The Flying Dutchman', a mainstay of maritime lore. It is a legendary ghost ship that is doomed to sail the oceans forever.

An alternative interpretation comes from a 19th-century dictionary that refers to the 'ghost of Jonah', a biblical seaman who supposedly brought bad luck to sailors. According to the Bible, God punished Jonah for his disobedience and he became the 'devil of the seas', after which the crew abroad his vessel killed him.

Another version of the Jonah, 'Duppy Johah'. The story refers the few days he spent inside a whale. This tale connects his days in the whale's tract with Davy Jones' Locker. *(Which itself is an idiom for the bottom of the sea. The resting place for drowned sailors and shipwrecks.)*

The Australians tell a tale of a fearsome pirate who sank to the bottom of the sea when crossing the equator and "now patrols the equator on his killer whale boarding any vessel that dares to pass the waters of the Kings Majestic Realm".

English sailors may believe his name is a corruption of 'Duffer Jones', a clumsy fellow who frequently found himself overboard.

The only time Davy comes to life is in the ceremony of crossing the line. Then he is usually impersonated by the smallest sailor on board, given a hump, horns and a tail, and his features made as ugly as possible. He is swinish, dressed in rags and seaweed, and shambles along in the wake of the sea king, Neptune, playing evil tricks upon his fellow sailors.

However, none of the stories is supported by credible evidence, so they remain tales told by old sea dogs. Thus, in many stories, Davy Jones is used as another name for Satan.

Davey Jones has been known to take on the role of Herald or Scribe on different occasions.

Chief Policeman

Policemen

The police are responsible for ensuring all pollywogs are accounted for and to bring them before King Neptune's court for sentencing.

They also keep order by containing the polliwogs, passing them to the bears after judgment and to 'arrest and return' any who try to escape the Bears.

Chief Bear

Bears

The bears' primary purpose is to control the Pollywogs during the 'dunking', the wet part of the ceremony.

There are always characters called Royal Bears, although they take different forms.

The Bears generally form the gauntlet through which the Pollywogs must run, and they are responsible for disciplining the pollywogs throughout the ceremony.

Their jobs include forcing the pollywogs heads underwater when they are dunked and placing pollywogs in the stocks

If a Pollywog disobeys an order, the Bears may use ores and paddles to beat them along with many insulting terms. The Bearss may also sit on Pollywogs in the tunnel and make them carry out various and sundry tasks.

Trident Stamper

The bearer of the king's trident

Secretary / The Royal Scribe

A task sometimes assigned to Davy Jones

Records the day's proceedings and read the register, ensuring all pollywogs undergo sentencing.

Barber

To 'shave' the Pollywogs

The Royal Baby

A relatively new addition to the Royal Navy's traditional range of players.

"Kissing the Royal Baby", calls for initiates to kneel before a member of the crew, who wears a mock diaper.

This "Baby" usually has a huge stomach covered with greasy materials ranging from cooking oil to mustard, shaving cream, eggs and oysters.

The Pollywogs must lick the Baby's navel area, while the "baby" grabs and shakes their head to better smear the goo onto their faces.

Doctor

To provide 'Medicine'. Such as foul-tasting paste pills and obnoxious liquids.

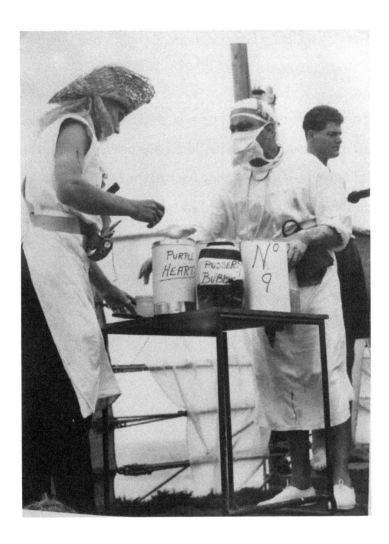

Pollywogs

The name 'pollywog' is from Middle English polwygle, made up of the elements pol = head and wiglen = to wiggle.

Similarly, 'tadpole' is from Middle English taddepol, made up of tadde = toad and again, pol = head. In modern English poll.

Having no hard parts, it might be expected that fossil tadpoles would not exist. However, traces of biofilms have been preserved and fossil tadpoles have been found dating back to the Miocene[9]. Tadpoles are eaten in some parts of the world and are mentioned in folk tales and used as a symbol in ancient Egyptian numerals.

---

[9] The Miocene is the first geological epoch of the Neogene Period and extends from about 23.03 to 5.333 million years ago

The Frog, a Poem, written by Hilaire Belloc.

Be kind and tender to the Frog,

And do not call him names,

As 'Slimy skin,' or 'Polly-wog,'

Or likewise 'Ugly James,'

Or 'Gap-a-grin,' or 'Toad-gone-wrong,'

Or 'Bill Bandy-knees':

The Frog is justly sensitive

To epithets like these.

No animal will more repay

A treatment kind and fair;

At least

so lonely people say

Who keep a frog (and, by the way,

they are extremely rare).

NOTE:

While the main and prime characters of this ceremony are regular, it has been known for some alterations, extras and additional characters to been seen, such as:

Lizards.

Wizard and Witch's

Tropicus and Ancient Dame

King Arthur

Mermaids

Dentist

Chaplain

There is and can be no end to the creative theatrical mind, nor should there be.

EVOLUTION

I have selected the following accounts of the Crossing the line Ceremony through the years.

These accounts are some of the most relevant, interesting, significant and well-documented examples of how the Crossing the Line ceremony has evolved over the last four to five hundred years

There is a significant lack of documented evidence from British seafarers, both before and since the formation of the Royal Navy, until much nearer our own era.

The main reason for this is twofold. The first is the British were not, by any stretch of the imagination, the first seamen to hold any passage of rites. The second, during both the great wars, documenting activities on Naval warships was not encouraged.

Regardless of nationality, the spread and basic ritual of the ceremony is almost identical and the progress and development seem shared by all seafarers.

Hence the inclusion of accounts from many nations' ships.

Chronologically presented, one can see how religion, cultural custom, social convention, trade and wars have influenced the development of this ritual.

HISTORIC ACCOUNTS

The first recognised documented account relating to the 'modern version' of the Crossing of the Line ceremony.

1529

In 1529 two French ships**, the Pensee,** of 200 tons and **the Sacre,** 120 tons, were bound for Sumatra.

Aboard were two brothers, Jean and Raoul Parmentier.

This voyage is well authenticated.

The ships sail from Dieppe on the 28th March 1529. They passed the Maldives and reached Ticou, in Sumatra, where Jean died of fever on the 3rd of December of that year.

During the voyage, Jean Parmentier wrote in his journal of the time the sailors took to celebrate the crossing of the line.

*"Le mardy XIme jour de may, au matin, furent faits chevaliers environ cin-quante de nos gens, et eurent chacun l'acollée en passant sous lequateur, etfut chantée la messe de Salve sancta parens à nottes pour la solennité du jour,et prismes un grand poisson nommé albacore et des bonnites, dont fut faitchaudière pour le souper en solennisant la fest de la chevalerie. "*10*

'There was a 'knighting' of sailors who had 'newly crossed'. The occasion was also marked with a meal of Albacore*11 and Bonitos,*12 followed by a celebration of Mass which included singing that "Was not a simple plainsong which might have been sung from memory. It was a choral work of a number of voices by some skilled composer."

---

10 Histoire d'vn voyage fait en la terre dv Brésil, avtrement dite Amérique... par Iean de Léry. [LaRochelle,] 1578.

11 Albacore is one of the smallest members of the tuna family. A highly migratory fish which roams the world's tropical and temperate oceans.

12 Bonito is a popular food fish in the Mediterranean; its flesh is like tuna and mackerel; its size is between the two.

1557

On the 4th of February, Frenchman Jean de Léry noted his [unnamed] ship, bound for Brazil crossed 'The centre of the World'.

"Cedit iour doncques quatrième de Feurier, que nous passasmes le Centre dumonde, les Matelots firët les ceremonies par eux accoustumees en ce tantfascheux & dangereux passage. Assauoir, de lier de cordes & plonger en mer,ou bien noircir & barbouiller le visage auec vn vieux drappeau frotté au culde la chaudière, ceux qui n'ôt iamais passé l'Équator pour les en fairesouuenir; toutesfois on se peut racheter & exempter de cela, côme ie fis, enleur payant le vin." [*]

De Léry documented the sailors took part, on what was a 'dangerous voyage', in a ceremony involved with "dunking sailors into the sea and blackening their faces with old flags which had been rubbed on the cauldron".

De Léry continued that, "those with no wish to participate could be exempt through a donation of money or wine".

The account of Jean de Léry is almost identical to ceremonies documented throughout the later periods of the 'Age of Sail'.

The actions of the sailors detailed in these two French accounts are very different, but the second, the report from De Léry, specifically mentions the ceremony is a 'tradition'.

How long it takes for an action to become a tradition is open to interpretation and speculation. But to suggest this ceremony was a tradition by 1557 poses many unanswered questions.

1577

Not all documented voyages which crossed the equator journaled a ceremony when crossing the equator. Possibly because the 'tradition' had not reached these countries sailors by the time of the chronicles?

For instance, the Reverend Master Francis Fletcher give plenty of detail in how Drake was out of sight of land for 63 days before; [**The Golden Hind**]

"Passing the fine equinoctiall, the 17th day. [February 1577]... Wee often met with aduerse winds, vnwelcome stormes, and to vs [at that time] lesse welcome calmes and being as it were in the bosome of the burning zone, weefelt the effects of sultring heat, not without the affrights of flashing lightnings and terrifyings of often claps of thunder."

One supposes if any religious or social ceremony had marked the crossing the "Preacher in this employment" would have told us?

1583

A fine example of a sixteenth-century ceremony is from the Dutchman, John Huygyen van Linschoten.

He travelled to the East Indies in 1583, crossing the equator on May the 26th of that year.

Unlike the account above, this ritual did not involve the dunking of sailors into the sea. It was more like a formal dinner party.

His diary entry reads:

'Crossed the line May 26; on May 29 (Whitsunday) the sailors chose an "Emperour among themselves' as was the "ancient custom".

After changing, 'all the officers in the ship' they held a feast which lasted for 3-4 days.

An argument broke out and rapiers and swords are drawn. They would not listen to the Captain, who was knocked to the deck.

The 24. of Aprill we fell upon the coaste of Guinea, which beginneth at nine degrees, and stretcheth untill wee come under the Equinoctiall, where wee have much thunder, lightning, and many showers of raine, with stormes of wind, which passe swiftly over, & yet fall with such force, that at every shower we are forced to strike sayle, and let the maine yeard fall to the middle of the mast, and many times cleane down, sometimes ten or twelve times every day: there wee finde a most extreame heate, so that all the water in the ship stinketh, whereby men are forced to stop their noses when they drinke, but when wee are past the Equinoctiall it is good againe, and the nearer wee are unto the land, the more it stormeth, raineth, thundreth and calmeth: so that most commonly the shippes are at the least two monthes before they can passe the line: . . .

The 26 of May wee passed the Equinoctiall line which runneth through the middle of the Hand of Saint Thomas, by the coast of Guinea, and then wee began to see the south star, and to loose the north star, and founde the sunne at twelve of the clocke at noone to be in the north, and after that we had a south east [wind, called a] general wind, which in those partes bloweth all the yeare through.

The 29 of May being Whitsonday, the ships of an ancient custome, doe use to chuse an Emperour among themselves, and to change all the officers in the ship, and to hold a great feast, which continueth three or foure days together, which wee observing chose an Emperour, and being at our banket, by meanes of certaine words that passed out of some of their mouthes, there fell great strife and contention among us, which proceeded so farre, that the tables were throwne downe and lay on the ground, and at the least a hundred rapiers drawne, without respecting the Captaine or any other, for he lay under foote, and they trod upon him, and had killed each other, and thereby had cast the ship away, if the Archbishop had not come out of his chamber among them, willing them to cease, where with they stayed their hands, who presently commaunded every man on paine of death, that all their Rapiers, Poynyardes, and other weapons should bee brought into his chamber, which was done, whereby all thinges were pacified, the first and principall beginners being punished and layd in irons, by which meanes they were quiet.[*13]

If it was not for the Archbishop who stepped in to stop the fight, they might have killed each other. Those who started it was punished and put in irons.

Note that Van Linschoten calls this an *'ancient custom'*. Although there is no trail of accounts to lead to an origin.

---

[13] The voyage of John Huyghen van Linschoten to the East Indies. From the old English translation of 1598.

1642

On the 16th of August 1642, we sailed from Stockholm, on board the [Dutch] ship **Fame**.

The Dutch ship 'Fame' was, in 1643 sailing along the coast of Portugal. On August the 24th, at or about mid-day, the ship's company performed a ceremony of tropical baptism, according to Thomas Campanius Holm.

"as is the custom with seamen when they cross the equinoctial line, to dip into the water those who have never crossed before."

What this particular 'Tropical baptism' entailed we shall never know as Holm did not record many details. This is our first recorded performance for the crossing of the Tropic of Cancer rather than the equator. However, just because accurate records are scarce does not mean this ceremony was not already established.

1645

The writer of the following is a member of the Order of Preaching Friars.

The only omission from this friar's diary is he does not name the ship he is sailing upon.

I will say, gentlemen, that it is an unbroken rule for all that have never passed the Ras Blanchards [Pointe du Raz], the Peak of the Canaries, Cape Blanc, or the Tropics or the equator, at each of those places to be baptised by a cupful of seawater dashed on his bare head.

This form of baptism is in the way of paying homage to or recognition of Neptune as if asking him then and there to calm the waves and give us favouring winds to let us pass with no danger; for these places are dangerous to approach, really prickly.

I feel these ceremonies are rather real bits of idolatry than prayers to God. We have grown used to such performances as reminders of our having passed those places; and in our staging of such ceremonies, really tom fooleries.

I should not fail to speak about them as necessary on long voyages, though it annoys me to blacken white paper with the tale of such excesses. They are planned and aimed at nothing more than making fun for the participants, to whom you have to give something like bottles of brandy or some other ardent liquor; which with us is divided among the ship's messes by sevens, five by the English, three by the Flemings and others.

Nobody can escape, not even the captain or the pilot, unless he has gone through it before. When staging the baptising they blacken your face by a cross smudged on from the soot on the bottom of the kettle. Stingy fellows are trussed up tightly with ropes and then a sailor seated on a gun carriage empties on them, drop by drop, on the left arm, a whole tank full of seawater and after an hour or so it congeals his blood, brings on shivers all over and trembling of all his members too severe for me to tell about.

Out of curiosity I wanted to undergo such a punishment, and as result, I have something never to forget, even if it is ludicrous and unfitting.[*14]

In this account the drop-by-drop torture is unusual and I wonder if the text really means to say that whenever you passed the Raz, (*the exit from the English Channel*), or the Peak of the Canaries or Cape Blanche this full ordeal was always inflicted?

---

[14] Guillaume Coppier. Histoire et voyage des Indes Occidentales; et deplusieurs autres regions maritimes et esloignées, diuisé en deux liures. Lyon, 1645.

1667

This reveals the first account of such a ceremony on a Portuguese ship.

It was diarised by two Italian Capuchins [friars] of fifteen, who boarded a ship in Lisbon, destined for the Congo via Brazil. (Yes, a strange passage, but there you are).

Favourable winds helped a speedy passage from Lisbon, taking only three months. Calms near the equator, however, held them up and gave unbearable heat for fifteen long August days.

The friars write: *"The Portuguese have an old tradition of having some entertainment when crossing the line. They take that day off to ask God for a safe voyage. Those who have never made the crossing must pay to the others or give them something to eat and drink. An act even us friars are obliged to do. Our rosaries and statues of saints made some money for the reading of masses for souls in the purgatory.*

If someone does not have the means forward this tribute, he is tied up by sailors dressed as officers and presented to a court presided by a sailor dressed in a cape. The judge hears him and condemns him to

be dipped three times in the sea by tying him strongly in a cable."[*15]

---

[15] Michel Ange de Gattine, & Denys de Carli de Plaisance. Relationcvrievse et nouvelle d'un voyage de Congo. Fait es années. 1666 &1667. Lyon, 1680.

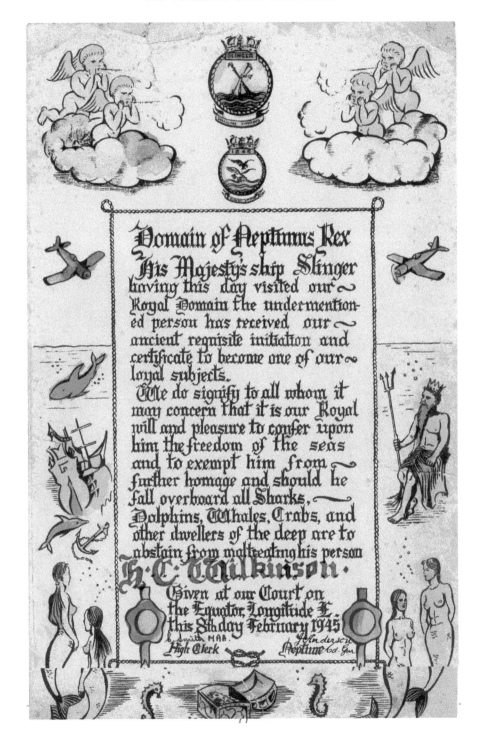

These images are supplied by the Royal Navy Research Archives

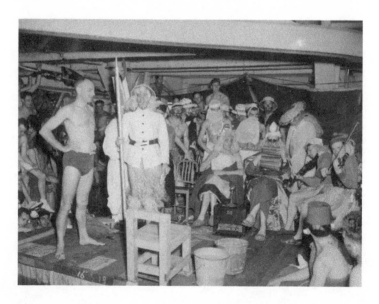

The following photographs were supplied by Andrew Alderson.

They were taken by his uncle, Edmund Alderson who sadly crossed the bar in 2018.

Andrew says,

"I have dug out the album and can say the following.

They were taken in 1964 onboard HMS Tiger during the Special Squadron Cruise. I have attached a copy of a map to this showing the route.

The ceremony was Oct 1964 in the Pacific Ocean.

There are only two photos with details on the back.

This one says Commander (in white) on the back.

This one says Skipper (dark top)."

I have used one of the photographs supplied by Andrew as the cover image for this book, Neptune and the Pollywogs.

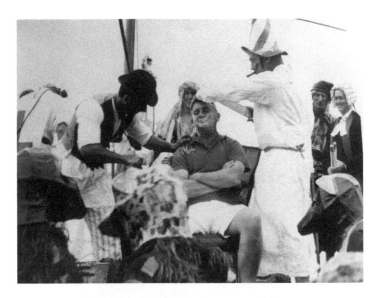

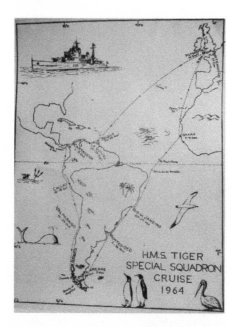

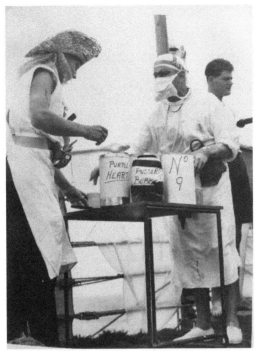

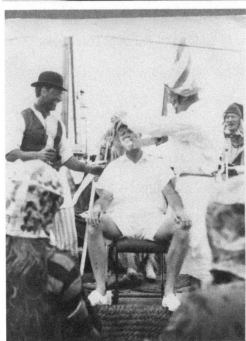

1708

On August the 2nd two ships, **the Duke** and **the Duchess**, sailed from Bristol under warrant to privateer, against the French and Spanish, from the Lord high admiral and her majesty Queen Elizabeth.

On September the 25th, the ships passed over the equator, heading for Cape Verde. This is a brief, but a descriptive account of that crossing the line ceremony. This day, according to custom, we duck'd those that had never pass'd the Tropick before. The manner of doing it was by a Rope thro a Block from the Main-Yard, to hoist 'em above half way up to the Yard and let 'em fall at once into the Water; having a Stick cross thro their Legs, and well fastened to the Rope, that they might not be surprised and let go their hold. This prov'd of great use to our fresh-water Sailors, to recover the Colour of their Skins which were grown very black and nasty. Those that we duck'd after this manner three times, were about 60, and others that would not undergo it, chose to pay Half a Crown Fine; the Mony to be levy'd and spent at a publick Meeting of all the Ships Companys, when we return to England. The Dutch Men and some English Men desir'd to be duck'd, some six, others eight, ten, and twelve times, to have the better Title for being treated when they come home.[*16]

---

[16] Woodes Rogers. A cruising voyage round the world. London, 1712.

1768

By the eighteenth century, there were well-established line-crossing rituals in the Royal Navy.

On the Endeavour, captained by James Cook in 1768, Joseph Banks noted how the crew created a list of everyone on board, including the cats and dogs. All were as to whether they had previously crossed the equator.

If they had not each must give their allowance of wine for four days or undergo a ducking ceremony. According to Banks, many were ducked into the Pacific Ocean three times. Some Banks said were "grinning and exulting in their hardiness", others "were almost suffocated."

25th. Oct. 1768. This morning at about eight o'clock we crossed the equinoctial line in about 33 W. from Greenwich, at the rate of four knots, which our seamen said was uncommonly good, the thermometer standing at 79°.

(The thermometers used in this voyage are two of Mr Bird's making, after Fahrenheit's scale, and seldom differ by more than a degree from each other, and that only when they are as high as 80°, in which case the mean reading of the two instruments is set down)

This evening the ceremony of ducking the ship's company was performed, as is always customary on crossing the line, when those who have crossed it before claim a right of ducking all that have not. The whole of the ceremony I shall describe.

About dinner-time a list was brought into the cabin containing the names of everybody and thing aboard the ship, (in which the dogs and cats were not forgotten); to this was fixed a signed petition from the ship's company de-siring leave to examine everybody in that list, that it might be known whether or not they had crossed the line before.

This was immediately granted, every-body being called upon the quarter-deck and examined by one of the lieutenants who had crossed the line: he marked every name either to be ducked or let off as their qualification directed.

Captain Cook and Dr Solander were on the blacklist, as were I myself, my servants and dogs for all of whom I was obliged to compound by giving the duckers a certain quantity of brandy, for which they willingly excused us the ceremony.

Many of the men, however, chose to be ducked rather than give up four day's allowance of wine, which was the price fixed upon, and as for the boys, they are always ducked, of course, so that about twenty-one underwent the ceremony.

A block was made fast to the end of the main-yard, and a long line reved through it, to which three pieces of wood were fastened, one of which was put between the legs of the man who was to be ducked, and to this he was tied very fast, another was for him to hold in his hands, and the third was over his head, lest the rope should be hoisted too near the block, and by that means the man be hurt.

When he was fastened upon this machine the boatswain gave the command by his whistle, and the man was hoisted up as high as the cross-piece over his head would allow, when another signal was made, and immediately the rope was let go, and his own weight carried him down; he was then immediately hoisted up again, and three times served in this manner, which was every man's allowance. Thus, ended the diversion of the day, for the ducking lasted until almost night, and sufficiently diverting it was to see the different faces that were made on this occasion, some grinning and exulting in their hardiness, whilst others were almost suffocated, and came up ready enough to have compounded after the first or second duck, had such a proceeding been allowable.

1774

We are now fairly under the Tropick and are preparing for a farce that is played on this occasion by every ship that goes to or fro under the Tropick. It is, it seems, a sort of Mason word, and till I am admitted in form, I must not appear to know it. I shall therefore only tell you that we have been made to expect a visit from old Tropicus and his ancient dame. He is a wizard and shea witch who inhabit an invisible Island in these Seas and have a privilege of raising contributions from every Ship that passes their dominions, only however from such as never was that way before.

But my account is cut short by the appearance of the Actors, who are dressed for their parts. Tropicus is performed by an old rough dog of a Tar, who needs very little alteration to become a callaban in mind and body, but his wife is played by a very handsome fellow, who is completely transformed.

Everybody is below waiting, in trembling expectation, and no wonder, for an awful ceremony this Visitation is. Tropick the Island was no sooner seen, than the Jolly boat [see note] was taken down, on pretence of going with the Captain aboard it to meet him, but in fact to be filled full of pump water for a use you shall hear by and by. This being done Tropick is spoke to thro' the trumpet, and a hollow voice demands what strangers are aboard. All this the people below hear, and tho' many of them.

Emigrants appear sensible, yet all the Highlanders and Islanders are so superstitious, that they may be easily imposed on, in such a thing as this; and they were completely so. The wizard now ordered them to be brought up, one by one blindfolded and their hands bound behind them; such was their fear, that they suffered this to be done without dispute.

In this situation, they were to answer certain questions which he put to them; if they spoke strictly truth, then he shaved them, took a small gratuity for his trouble, gave them his benediction, and let them pass. But if they disguised or concealed the truth, which he was supposed perfectly to know, then he tumbled them into the Sea, where they perished.

Prepossessed with this idea, a poor lad was brought before the infernal Judge:

"Answer me," said he sternly, *"answer me the truth; what made you leave home?"*

"O troth sir, I dinna well ken:"

"But you must know," said he, *"so answer me instantly."*

"O Dear, O Lord! I think it was because so many were going, I did not like to stay behind,"

"And pray what are you good for in this world, to prevent me sending you to the next?"

"Trouth, an please your honour, e'en, very little."

"What," said he, with a voice like thunder, *"are you good for nothing?"*

"O yes, yes, I am no very ill at the small fishing."

As this young man did not seem to overrate his own merits, the wizard was satisfied, placed him on the side of the boat, which he believed was the ship, being still blindfolded and bound.

The wizard began to shave him with a notched stick and pot-black. The sharp notches soon brought blood, and the poor devil starting from the pain, tumbled into the boat amongst the water, and thinking it the sea, roared with terror.

And in this consisted the whole wit of the entertainment.

He was now unbound and restored to the light and as keen to bring in his neighbours, who one by one, went thro' the same operation. As soon as it was over, the custom licences the sailors to treat the officers with every degree of freedom, nor do they fail to take the opportunity.

The Cap', mates, supercargo, and all were chaced round and round and drenched in the water from the boat, which they threw at them in bucket-fulls.

We had now gone to the Cabin, and believed all was over, when a loud screaming on deck brought us up to see what was the matter, and we found our Cap' had begun to act a tragedy after our comedy, and to oblige these poor ruined creatures to pay five shillings for each, or be pulled up to a mast and from that plunged down to the Sea.

This was a sum impossible to be raised, and the poor women were running with what remained of their clothes to give in place of it to save their husbands and fathers. Amongst others Marion was going with all speed, with her aunt's poplin gown; but it was needless, for John Lawson now stood at bay, his fist clinched and swearing by the great God, that the first man that touched him had not another moment to live, nor was there one hardy enough to encounter a fist, which had not its fellow on board.

But this was not the case with others, and they had one man tied, and only waited to see, if his wife had as many moveables as to save his life, for he was a poor weak old man, and would not have agreed with this method of bathing. I never in my life saw my brother in such a passion; he swore solemnly, that the moment he got to land, he would raise a prosecution agaist the Cap', who pleaded that it was the custom, and only intended as a little drink money to the sailors.

If that is the case, replied my brother, let them give up then cloths, and they shall be satisfied. This was complied with cheerfully, he gave them what they were satisfied with, to which they returned three cheers, as he went to the cabin and serenaded us with the favourite song;

O grog is the liquor of life

The delight of each free British tar.

O grog is the liquor of life

The delight of each free British tar.

Notes:

"The jolly boat was generally swung at the stern of the vessel. Regarding the 'awful ceremony,' John Luffman, author of A Brief Account of the Island of Antigua. 1789, who made the voyage from the Downs to Antigua in 1786, says;

"I had almost forgot to observe that on passing the tropic of Cancer, the custom of ducking and shaving such as have not before crossed it, was performed by the seamen with some humour on one man and two boys. The passengers waved the ceremony by a liquor fine."

Note:

As for *"satisfied"* in the last sentence:

"Meaning that if the sailors would give up their claim to the clothes of the emigrants, he (Mr Schaw) would pay for their grog."*17

---

17 Journal of a lady of quality; being the narrative of a journey from Scot-land to the West Indies, North Carolina, and Portugal, in the years 1774to 1776. The original manuscript is Egerton 2423 of the British Museum.

1777

HMS Proteus, of 1777 was a 26-gun sixth rate. When she was passing through the strait of Macassar near Borneo, it is confirmed by this date that 'crossing the line' was an established procedure. The report adds to the ceremony an act, in which the God Neptune's guard, *"by tradition dressed as Moorish soldiers"* appear.

"King Neptune is preceded by a large sailor of mixed race and followed by a judge, writer, a hairdresser and his apprentice, a priest and his helper, four bailiffs, and the Devil with a large tail and dressed in sheep's skins. These characters have the task of forming the aforementioned court."

At the end of the parade appears King Neptune himself and his sons. Neptune then takes the captain's seat and starts giving silly orders, while one of his guards takes the helm, the other guards watch over the officers.

The priest's helper takes the donations before the judge and the priest removes their clothes revealing women's clothing underneath and start silly dancing with the hairdresser and his apprentice to the sound of ridiculous music."

1808

The earliest story by an American...

As we were now approaching the equinoctial line, being in 12° north latitude, the wind became lighter, and I heard a faint buzzing among the old salts about the visit of old Neptune to his children, which I then believed was no farce, until ocular demonstration convinced me otherwise, as will hereafter be shown.

January 3rd... We braced up our yards on the larboard tack; and as we expected to cross the line the next night, preparations were being made for the reception of old Neptune, such as dressing two of the oldest sailors to personate him and his wife; throwing over a tar barrel on fire; and hailing the sea-god from on board.

All this buffoonery was performed after dark, and so managed as to be kept a secret from the green hands.

And here I must not omit to state, that this foolery was sanctioned by the captain and officers, very much to their mortification afterwards, as the scene of confusion which ensued had like to have closed with a mutiny.

On the next morning, *the 8th*, the play began; the green hands were confined in the forecastle, one at a time being sent up blindfolded, who was then received by his majesty of the sea, and the operation of shaving commenced.

The lather consisted of slush mixed with the dirty water of the grindstone tub; the razor was a piece of old iron hoop: the face being well be smeared with this lather, the work of shaving commenced, during which his majesty puts some interrogatories, such as,

"Do you intend to become a member of my family and a faithful subject of my realm?" &c.

When the mouth is opened to give the answer, it is crammed full of odoriferous lather. This done, he is well scraped with the hoop and ducked with salt water, and then let off to enjoy the remainder of the farce.

I recollect, when they were about to cram the delicious lather into my mouth, I struck the man who held it, and in the bustle, the bandage fell from my eyes, and I discovered the whole trick.

A scene of confusion here took place; the green hands all sided together and determined not to submit to the operation, and the old sailors attempting to force us to yield, a riot took place, which was not, without much difficulty, quelled by die officers.

Order being at length restored, and the crew having returned to their duty, all was soon forgotten.[*18]

---

[18] George Little. Life on the ocean; or, twenty years at sea. Boston, 1846

1814

A few days before the last storms, we crossed the tropical line. On crossing it, the usual ceremonies were gone through with on board our schooner. I say usual because the practice was one which was never omitted; but I learn that it is now not so common on board of American vessels and I hope that the good sense and intelligence of all masters, will lead them to do away with the cruel and barbarous practice. It is a custom more honoured in the breach than in the observance.

As we drew near the line, a hoarse, rough voice hailed us, with the salutation of 'Schooner ahoy! What schooner's that!' To this our captain replied,

Giving the name of the vessel, where from, where bound, and the name of the commander. The same rough voice then commanded us to heave-to, and he would come on board of us.

The sails were then laid to the masts, and Neptune, his wife, barber, and a numerous retinue, came up over the bows and passed along into the waist, where the captain stood ready to welcome them on board. The ocean-god and the fair Amphitrite were rigged out in the most grotesque and fantastical manner possible. The whole was a burlesque on the description of Spenser:

"First came great Neptune, with his three-forked mace that rules the seas and makes them rise or fall; His dewey locks did drop with brine apace. Under his diadem imperiall; And by his side his queene with coronall, Fair Amphitrite."

The imperial diadem was made of duck, covered with oakum; the three-forked mace was a fish spear; his majesty's robe of state was a red baize shirt, and on his shoulders were a massive pair of epaulettes, made of tarred oakum.

The fair Amphitrite was a strapping great sailor, rigged out in the queerest toggery in which female grace and loveliness were ever burlesqued. The landsmen were all placed in the waist; and his majesty, with a nice discrimination, remembered the faces of all who had ever been welcomed into his realm. But the old god was for once in his life at fault. It will be perceived that I had crossed the tropic and also the equator before; but my first captain was a man of too much good taste, and gentlemanly feelings, to permit old Neptune to come on board his ship.

I had heard the ceremony of shaving so often described by sailors, that I was au fait to the thing; and my answers to the queries that had been propounded to me for several days before we reached the tropic, were very satisfactory.

I had secured the silence of an old weather-beaten and rum-loving tar, who was with me in the ship, by giving him, during the whole cruise, my allowance of grog. I passed, therefore, for an affiliated and matriculated one.

The candidates having been selected, the process of shaving was now to commence.

Our boat was placed on the deck, half-filled with water, and a plank placed across it, but in a ticklish manner. The candidate being blindfolded, was conducted to, and made to seat himself on the plank, when several questions were propounded to him, which, if he was indiscreet enough to answer, as soon as his mouth was open, a brush, filled with tar, blacking, slush, and all manner of filth, was thrust in.

After they had worried their poor victim for some time in this manner, they proceeded to lather him, by smearing his face all over with the same detestable compound; and he was then scraped with a piece of iron hoop, notched to make it more effective, until his face was lacerated to such a degree that the blood oozing out, mingling with the tar and filth, gave the poor ill-used landsman a most deplorable appearance.

To conclude the ceremony, one end of the plank was slipped away, and he received two or three severe duckings in the not over cleanly water.

Those who betrayed any signs of resistance or indignation fared the worst — while those who took the thing quietly, and passed it off as a good joke, got off with a light penalty.

One of our young landsmen, with a regard to the economy of his dress, which he rightly enough anticipated would not be very sacred against the lathering of the rough barber, had stripped himself to his browsers; but while he preserved his shirt and jacket clean, his raw hide had to suffer; for he was lathered and shaved from his head down to his waist; and it was many days, by the application of grease, and soap and water, assisted by a stiff scrubbing brush, before he got his body again in a decent plight.

No one, save myself, who had not before been shaved, escaped — but some who were so liberal as to bribe high with grog, got off with little annoyance.

Our lite craft, for a while, presented the picture of a Pandemonium, in which the demons were holding a Saturnalia; and it was not until the next day, that the actors in this rude ceremony were sober enough to do their duty.

After all, had been thus roughly welcomed, and Neptune and his retinue had spliced the main-brace with all the grog they could get, they retired the same way they came — the royal Amphitrite as unamiably

After all, had been thus roughly welcomed, and Neptune and his retinue had spliced the main-brace with all the grog they could get, they retired the same way they came — the royal Amphitrite as unamiably drunk, as was her loving spouse, they wished us a successful and happy cruise —and we kept on our way.*[19]

---

[19] The yarn of a Yankee privateer by Benjamin Frederick Browne. Funk & Wagnalls Company, 1926.

1832

*Captain Robert FitzRoy of **HMS Beagle** suggested the practice had developed from earlier ceremonies in Spanish, Portuguese, and Italian vessels passing notable headlands.*

He thought it was beneficial to morale.

A ceremony took place during the second survey voyage of HMS Beagle.

On the evening of 16 February 1832, a pseudo-Neptune hailed the ship. Those credulous enough to run forward to see Neptune "were received with the watery honours which it is customary to bestow". The officer on watch reported a boat ahead, and Captain FitzRoy ordered: "hands up, shorten sail".

Using a speaking trumpet, he questioned Neptune, who would visit them about 9am the next day, the novices or "griffins" were assembled in the darkness and heat of the lower deck, then one at a time were blindfolded and led up on deck by "four of Neptune's constables", as "buckets of water were thundered all around".

The first "griffin" was **Charles Darwin**, who noted in his diary how he...

"was then placed on a plank, which could be easily tilted up into a large bath of water. — They then lathered my face & mouth with pitch and paint & scraped some of it off with a piece of roughened iron hoop. —a signal being given I was tilted head over heels into the water, where two men received me & ducked me. —at last, glad enough, I escaped. — most of the others were treated much worse, dirty mixtures being put in their mouths & rubbed on their faces. — The whole ship was a shower bath: & water was flying about in every direction: of course, not one person, even the Captain, got clear of being wet through."

Note;

FitzRoy quoted Otto von Kotzebue's 1830 description in his 1839 Narrative of the Surveying Voyages of His Majesty's Ships Adventure and Beagle between the Years 1826 and 1836.

1832

The strange and almost savage ceremonies used at sea on crossing the equator have been so often described that a voyager, at this time of day, may be well excused for omitting any minute account of such wild proceedings. The whole affair, indeed, is preposterous in its conception, and, I must say, brutal in its execution.

 Notwithstanding all this, however, I have not only permitted it to go on in ships which I commanded, but have even encouraged it, and set it agoing, when the men themselves were in doubt. Its evil is transient if any evil there be, while it certainly affords Jack a topic for a month beforehand and a fortnight afterwards; and if so ordered as to keep its monstrosities within the limits of strict discipline, which is easy enough, it may even be made to add to the authority of the officers, instead of weakening their influence.

In a well-regulated ship, within one hour from the time when these scenes of riot are at their height, order is restored, the decks are washed and swabbed up, the wet things are hung on the clothes' lines between the masts to dry; and the men, dressed in clean trousers and duck frocks, are assembled at their guns for muster, as soberly and sedately as if nothing had happened to discompose the decorous propriety of the ship's discipline.

The middies, in like manner, may safely be allowed to have their own share of this rough fun, provided they keep as clear of their immediate superiors as the ship's company keep clear of the young gentlemen. And I must do the population of the cockpit the justice to say, that, when they fairly set about it, maugre their gentleman-like habits, aristocratical sprinklings, and the march of intellect to boot, they do contrive to come pretty near to the honest folks before the mast in the article of ingenious ferocity.

The captain, of course, and, generally speaking, all the officers keep quite aloof, pocketing up their dignity with vast care, and ready, at a moment's warning, to repress any undue familiarity. As things proceed, however, one or two of the officers may possibly become so much interested in the skylarking scenes going forward as to approach a little too near, and laugh a little too loud, consistently with the preservation of the dignity of which they were so uncommonly chary at first starting.

It cannot be expected, and indeed is not required, that the chief actors in these wild gambols, stripped to the buff, and shying buckets of water at one another, should be confined within very narrow limits in their game. Accordingly, some mount the rigging to shower down their cascades, while others squirt the fire-engine from unseen corners upon the head of the unsuspecting passer-by. And if it so chances, I say chances, that any one of the "commissioned nobs" of the ship shall come in the way of these explosions, it is served out to him like a thunder-storm, "all accidentally," of course.

Well; what is he to do? He feels that he has indiscreetly trusted himself too far; and even if he has not actually passed the prescribed line, still he was much too near it, and the offence is perhaps unintentional. At all events, it is of too trifling a nature and, under the peculiar circumstances of the moment, to make a complaint to the captain would be ridiculous. Having, therefore, got his jacket well wet, and seeing the ready means of revenging himself in kind, he snatches up a bucket, and, forgetting his dignity, hurls the contents in the face of the mid who has given him a sousing but two seconds before!

From that moment his commission goes for nothing, and he becomes, for the time being, one of the biggest Billy-boys amongst them.

The captain observing him in this mess shrugs his shoulders, walks aft, muttering,

"It's all your own fault, Mr.Hailtop; you've put yourself amongst these mad younkers; now see how they'll handle you!"

Nothing, I confess, now looks to me more completely out of character with our well-starched discipline than a "staid lieutenant" romping about the booms, skulling up the rigging, blowing the grampus, and having it blown upon him by a parcel of rattle pated reefers.

But I remember well in the Volage being myself so gradually seduced by this animating spectacle of fun, that, before I knew where I was, I had crossed the rope laid on the deck as a boundary between order and disorder, and received a bucket of cold water in each ear, while the spout of a fire-engine, at the distance of two feet, was playing full in my eyes. On turning my head round to escape these cataracts, and to draw breath, a tar-brush was rammed half-way down my throat!

Far different was the scene, and very different, of course, my deportment, four or five years afterwards on the same spot, when, instead of being the junior lieutenant, I was the great gun of all, the mighty master-nob of the whole party, that is to say, the captain himself.

I was then in command of **the Lyra,** a ten-gun sloop-of-war; and after the shaving operations were over, and all things put once more in order, I went on board the **Alceste** frigate to dine with my excellent friend and commanding officer, the late Sir Murray Maxwell.

Lord Amherst, the ambassador to China, was on board, and in great glee with the sight of what had been enacted before him; for although, as I have always said, these scenes are not of a nature to bear agreeable description, they certainly are amusing enough to see — for once.

We soon sat down to dinner; and there was, of course, a great deal of amusement in telling the anecdotes of the day, and describing Father Neptune's strange aspect, and his still stranger-looking family and attendants. I ventured to back one of my figures against all or any of theirs, if not for monstrosity, at least for interest of another kind.*[20]

---

[20] The Lieutenant and Commander;Fragments of voyages and travels by Lieutenant and Commander Basil Hall. 1862

1841

No date, but probably late November or early December.

We had a shipmate once named 'Jack Nastyface,'. His face was as rough as a macadamised road.

The first time we crossed the equator, in the Pacific, "Jack" was at the masthead looking out for whales.

As soon as 'eight bells' were struck 'Jack. was relieved. He was informed we had crossed the line.

'Jack' never would be behind anybody in intelligence.

"The devil we did!" says, Jack. "Can't ye tell us some news? didn't I see it as well as you did and better too? wasn't I aloft? I saw the line before any man aboard."[21]

---

[21] Richard Tobias Greene, the Sandusky Mirror, January 13, 1855.

1858

A tale from a Russian ship

On the 18th of January 1858 advancing at a creeping pace, we finally reached the equator.

The event was celebrated in an appropriate fashion.

As luck would have it, it was Sunday. All the flags were turned into costumes. A throne, draped with red pennants, was set up near the smokestack. At four o'clock, to the accompaniment of a drum, a tambourine and an accordion, a procession started from the crew's quarters.

It included a nude "Negro," blackened with soot and wearing a red Sasha Turk; a muzhik with a trained bear which was turning somersaults and cutting capers as instructed by his master.

There were also soldiers and a fantastic cook carrying ladles and sieves, and at last, Neptune himself, impersonated by the ship's wag Khudobin. The part of Neptune's spouse was played by Vaska, a stoker.

To the accompaniment of the wildest music, the procession made the round of the Clipper.

Finally, Neptune mounted the throne and was surrounded by his motley retinue. The first one to be presented to him was the captain, who made a contribution only for the ship since he had crossed the line before. The officers placed coins on a separate tray. All swore that they would never court a sailor's lawful wife.

The real fun began when the sailor's turn came.

Upon some, the sea god's disfavour was visited with special severity. A stream of water from a pump is no joking matter. Clerks and other folk whom seamen are not fond of had to suffer the most.

Half a dozen men held the victim down and in spite of all his efforts to avoid it, the water from the pump squirted right into his face and he was forced to swallow a good deal of salt water. The last ones to be thus treated were naturally Neptune himself and his spouse, who played their parts with resourcefulness and wit.

The day ended with songs and an extra glass of vodka.*[22]

---

[22] Vysheslavtsev. Essays on the pen and karandosh of the Circumnavigation, 1860.

1862

HMS Rifleman was a Rifleman-class wooden screw gun vessel launched in 1846 and sold in Hong Kong in 1869.

The following transcript is taken from a handwritten journal. [see image] Although I have attempted to interpret and transcribe the document accurately, there are a few words missing and a few omissions due to the condition of the document and the handwriting itself.

Account of the ceremony on crossing the line on board **HMS Rifleman** bound for China, March 6th, 1862.

His Majesty King Neptune hailed the ship and finding the usual trophies given on those occasions that he had some children on board, who had never been in his realm he observed he should be happy to receive them the next morning and hoped we should be ready for this reception.

The branch of lizards headed the procession after which marched the police, four *stables* and one of the medic's assistants *bray* who had crossed the line before, dressed an in a coat with large white buttons and canvass hats.

With the police came the glorious car of Neptune, dragged by 12 horses and covered with flags on which sat Neptune and Amphitrite, his wife and their two children.

Neptune and Amphitrite dressed in fantastic costumes with a profusion of *rope* for his beard. Of course, his majesty wore a crown.

He also carried a trident on which was a red herring spilled (*?*). The two children were dressed in red ochre, his Majesty was followed by his staff of barbers to shave you, Doctors to give you pills and bears to drown you.

All got up with the utmost disregard of escpense, *[expense]*. Well, one of the doctors has and quite a profession *alcoate* and used of his eye-glass in a respectable manner. The procession halted on the Quarter deck and condescended to drink a glass of unknown the *shipped* after which they retired to go their duties.

The policemen sent everyone below but those who crossed the line before, so as to have them up one by one. I was the first one had up – being blindfolded below, I was led on deck by two policemen – I had no sooner put any foot on deck than I was saluted by a deluge of water in my face and washed like a lamb to the slaughter.

I was taken before Neptune who interrogated me as to *any health* and ordered me a pill to keep me in good health. I was not so green enough to let him put it in my mouth.

I was then led on to the platform and being seated, the barbers most politely asked me whether I required shaving. It would have been all the same whether I had or not.

After having been shaved I was *troubled* on the awning and after having had a good dosing was free to help shave everyone else, which you may be sure I did.

We got the S E Trade on 8th March and left its 18th and arrived here, at the Cape of Good Hope. on 7th April.

We lost our foremost mast in a squall and we saw some Albatross and after having passed the S. E. trade.

We shall start about the 25th or 26th for Singapore and I hope I shall get a good lot of letters when I get there.

By the bye, I forgot to tell you I celebrated my birthday in the bay, by sending liquor to my messmate and wishing many happy returns.

We caught a shark the day before we cross the line.

1897

No ships name given, but the following is recorded by Mark Twain.

Sept 5th.

Closing in on the equator this noon. A sailor explained to a young girl that the ship's speed is poor because we are climbing up a bulge toward the centre of the globe; but that when we should once get over, at the equator and start down-hill, we should fly.

When she asked him the other day what the foreyard was, he said it was the front yard, the open area in the front end of the ship. That man has a good deal of learning stored up, and the girl is likely to get it all.

Afternoon.

Crossed the equator. In the distance, it looked like a blue ribbon stretched across the ocean. Several passengers kodak'd it.

We had no fool ceremonies, no fantastics, no horse-play. All that sort of thing has gone out.

In old times a sailor, dressed as Neptune, used to come in over the bows, with his suite and lather up and shave everybody who was crossing the equator for the first time and then cleanse these unfortunates by swinging them from the yard-arm and ducking them three times in the sea.

This was considered funny.

Nobody knows why.

No, that is not true. We do know why.

Such a thing could never be funny on land; no part of the old-time grotesque performances gotten up on shipboard to celebrate the passage of the line could ever be funny on shore — they would seem dreary and witless to shore people.

But the shore people would change their minds about it at sea, on a long voyage. On such a voyage, with its eternal monotonies, people's intellects deteriorate; the owners of the intellects soon reach a point where they almost seem to prefer childish things to things of a maturer degree. One is often surprised at the juvenilities which grown people indulge in a sea and the interest they take in them and the consuming enjoyment they get out of them.

This is on long voyages only.

The mind gradually becomes inert, dull, blunted; it loses its accustomed interest in intellectual things; nothing but horse-play can rouse it, nothing but wild and foolish grotesqueries can entertain it. On short voyages it makes no such exposure of itself; it hasn't time to slump down to this sorrowful level.*[23]

---

[23] Samuel Langhorne Clemens. Following the equator; a journey around the world. By Mark Twain. Hartford, Connecticut 1897

1910

On this voyage, we had a number of young people on board who were crossing the equator for the first time, so Neptune kindly offered to leave his ocean depths and to board the ship, in the good old-fashioned orthodox style to further these young folks' education.

Just as we crossed the Line, the ship was hailed from the sea, her name and destination were ascertained, and she was peremptorily ordered to heave to, Neptune naturally imagining that he was still dealing with sailing ships. The engines were at once stopped, and Neptune, with his Queen, his Doctor, his Barber, his Sea Bears and the rest of his Court, all in their traditional get-up, made their appearance on the upper deck, to the abject terror of some of the little children, who howled dismally at this alarming irruption of half naked savages with painted faces.

I myself enacted Neptune in an airy costume of fish scales, a crown, and a flowing beard and wig of bright sea-green. Of course, my Trident had not been forgotten. Amphitrite, my queen, was the star comedian of the South African music hall stage and the little man was really extraordinarily funny, keeping up one incessant flow of rather pungent gag and making the spectators roar with laughter.

All the traditional ceremonies and good-natured horseplay were scrupulously adhered to and some twenty schoolboys and five adults were duly dosed, lathered, shaved, hosed and then toppled backwards into a huge canvas tank of sea-water, where the boys persisted in swimming about in all their clothes.

The proceedings were terminated by Neptune and his entire Court following the neophytes into the tank, and I am afraid that we induced some half dozen male spectators to accompany us into the tank rather against their will, one old German absolutely fuming with rage at the unprecedented liberty that was being taken with him.[*24]

[24] Lord FredericHamilton. Here, there, and everywhere. New York. 1921

1920

H.M.S. Renown moved into the sultry waters of the tropics. Neptune came on board and he demanded the Royal victim with glee. The good fellowship of Osborne was called on now: the British capacity to grin through five minutes of discomfort. The Prince of Wales was docile while the courtiers of the Equatorial king sang:

> *Shave him and bash him,*
>
> *Duck him and splash him,*
>
> *Torture and smash him*
>
> *And don't let him go.*

The orders were carried out with brutal precision.[*25]

---

[25] Hector Bolitho. King Edward VIII. His life and reign. London, 1937 Reprinted with permission of Eyre & Spottiswoode, publishers.

1943/46

An interesting American tale.

I first crossed the equator aboard an LCI(L) —Landing Craft, Infantry (Large) — in late February or early March 1943, I forget which it was. We had an early type of LCI which in those days were awkward, uncomfortable vessels about 155 feet in length designed to transport some 100 or so troops onto the beach on amphibious assaults.

Ours had a complement of some 22 men and 3 officers in the ship's company, with two officer passengers, these two being connected with the LCI Flotilla Staff.

We were travelling in a convoy of about 32 ships, mostly LCIs, minesweepers and submarine chasers. Our point of crossing was on a more or less direct line between the Panama Canal and Bora Bora in the western group of the Society Islands.

We had discovered soon after leaving Norfolk that the entire ship's company was made up of pollywogs. Of the whole gang of us, only one officer passenger, a young lieutenant in the Supply Corps who had come up through the ranks, had ever been initiated into the mysteries of Crossing the Line. Needless to say, he filled our ears with all sorts of blood-curdling yarns about what we were about to face.

We allowed him to have his sport until it became tiresome to us and then pointed out to him that if he felt that he alone was going to play each role from King Neptune down to the Royal Baby while attempting to grease and clip a whole shipload of unwilling sailors, he had his work cut out for himself.

He, being a reasonable man, saw the logic of this and. except for uttering a few dark threats about seeing to it that we would not get our shellback certificates, he subsided and held his peace.

Consequently, the day we crossed the line we spent several hours lounging on the deck watching through binoculars the ordeals and torments being undergone by those no more inexperienced than ourselves who were merely unfortunate enough to find themselves aboard ships with strong shellback parties.

Later in the war and in connection with operations in New Guinea and the Philippines, I crossed the equator several times, but each time was aboard a ship that was crisscrossing back and forth regularly so that all hands were shellbacks several times over.

By the end of the war, I had crossed the equator about 6 times in each direction, and the nearest I had come to initiation was a few hundred yards while watching the ceremony through field glasses.

Therefore, I was greatly pleased in 1946 in connection with an Antarctic expedition (*Operation High jump)* to be on hand for and to participate in a bona fide Crossing the line Ceremony.

We crossed aboard the USCGC Northwind, an icebreaker, in mid-December on a great circle course from Panama to Scott Island in the Antarctic Ocean.

On the leg from Norfolk to Panama, the shellbacks had gotten together and been assigned our roles. Being a Naval Officer aboard a Coast Guard Cutter, I was automatically suspect and was assigned the role of Defense Attorney for the pollywogs — a position of some delicacy in that it sometimes happens that if the Defense Attorney makes too eloquent a plea, things may become so unruly that he finds himself subjected to various indignities along with his clients.

In Panama City, a delegation went ashore and purchased various costumes and trimmings, and the first few days at sea were spent in building a large open canvas water tank below and just aft of the helicopter flight deck. A straight-backed chair was secured to the flight deck by hinges on its back legs in such a fashion that an occupant thereof, after being treated by the Royal Barber, could be tipped over backwards and into the tank below where two stalwart shellbacks could supervise the ducking and presumably rescue the victim in his last extremity.

Also, a canvas tunnel was constructed about 15 feet long and leading up a well-greased ramp to the flight deck. Into this tunnel was led a series of high-pressure water hoses.

The main cast of characters consisted of such standard personalities as King Neptune, his Queen, the Royal Baby, an obese Petty Officer, the Royal Prosecutor, Defense Attorney, the Royal Jury, the Royal Physician and Dentist,with squirt guns filled with a very bitter fluid, the Royal Barber, and various others bounding and howling about.

We were all briefed in our duties by the Shellback Committee and were read instructions from the Navy Department cautioning us against committing any physical violence which might injure the initiates.

On the morning of the crossing, the pollywogs were stripped to their under-drawers and led aft one at a time, the higher officers going first in order to ensure they are getting well initiated while we were still full of pep and enthusiasm. Each person was first shoved into the tunnel, and as he tried to crawl along it, powerful streams of water harassed him each inch of the way.

He was then brought before the Royal Court and after bowing to the King and Queen and kissing the Royal Baby, was charged with a series of major crimes, the most serious of which was the fact that all during his life thus far he had failed to cross the equator.

As Defense Attorney, I took the position that although my client was guilty of everything charged to him and probably more besides, indeed deserved to be tossed over the side without more ado ,none the less I reluctantly pleaded for mercy, and asked the court merely to have the unfortunate criminal shorn, greased, baptised.

Officers and Petty Officers received individual attention from the Shellbacks, of course, but by the time the main mass of enlisted men came through, there were probably some 75 or more pollywogs, to begin with, representing about half the ship's company, the first bloom of enthusiasm had worn off and the men were run through in groups in rather haphazard fashion.

All in all, everyone had a merry time of it, and it was several days before the grease had been properly cleaned from the decks and several weeks before the ship's barber was able to restore any sort of order to the haircuts of those who had been treated by the Royal Barber.

I should mention the first to go through the initiation was our Commanding Officer, Captain Charles W. Thomas, USCG. A rather violent initiation was planned for him, but at the last minute the Shellbacks got cold feet and sent a delegation to the "old man" to say that if he preferred, he would be given only a perfunctory initiation. Captain Thomas, a wonderful gentleman and a good sport in every respect, insisted emphatically that he be spared not one whit. Indeed, he entered into the spirit of the game wholeheartedly, harangued the court, made speeches to one and all, took his initiation in extremely good grace, and after washing and dressing, joined in the remaining festivities — now as a certified shellback — with great vigour and enthusiasm.[*26]

---

[26] Manuscript statement from William Gerrish Metcalf, dated December10, 1953

HMS DEER SOUND

The following images are the detailed account of the crossing the line ceremony of HMS Deer Sound on the 7th of February 1945[27].

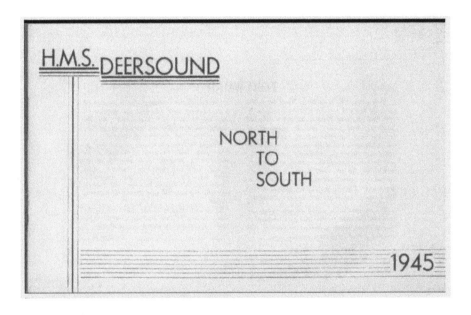

FOREWORD

Very infrequently, in the Royal Navy, does a ship cross the line with only 69 of a ship's company of over 600 who were Freemen, but this actually did occur in "Deer Sound," and the opportunity of initiating these landlubbers into the mysteries of the sea, although a formidable enterprise, seemed too tempting to be ignored. Admittedly it was war time, and the Service demands that constant watch be kept, but for one day who could disapprove if the daily routine was relaxed and the time-honoured custom performed? That this decision was justified and that the ceremony was a complete success is undoubted.

It is therefore at the request of many officers and men that this small brochure has been compiled, to serve as a permanent account of an enjoyable and certainly a most interesting experience.

Under the existing conditions, it was at first doubtful if any ceremony could take place and arrangements could only be made at the last moment. Notwithstanding, the organisation was noted for its completeness, originality and smoothness of execution.

It would be impossible to name all those who, by their energies and co-operation, contributed to the success of the ceremony, but of these Mr. Watts, W.S.O., R.N., must surely take precedence. Many others, especially the A.E.O.'s and Shipwrights' Departments, ably assisted, for without their help the ceremony must have fallen far short of the high level attained.

So, in spite of all restrictions, and trusting in her famous motto, "Virtuti non armis fido," "Deer Sound" carried out the ancient laws of the sea.

L.R.R.

Page Two

THE CEREMONY OF CROSSING THE LINE AS CARRIED OUT ON BOARD H.M.S. "DEER SOUND" ON THE 7th FEBRUARY, 1945.

THE origin of the Crossing of the Line Ceremony is somewhat obscure—but it has been the practice of Seamen, and especially British Seamen, to observe these rites for some hundreds of years. The ceremony probably dates back to the Vikings, who carried out some form of ritual before arriving at Gibraltar and always before crossing the 30 deg. of latitude. In that time the Equator as such was hardly known, and it was a legend that the Earth was encircled by a serpent. In order to propitiate this reptile certain rites had to be observed. The combination of these rites and those of the old Vikings appear to have resulted in the present and modern form of "Crossing the Line."

The ceremony has now become recognised, and is one of the many functions all of which go to make the numerous laws of the sea. To the professional sailor these laws are very real, and their non-observance or treatment in an offhand manner may bring bad luck to his ship.

It was, with full regard to these superstitions, and with a real sense of their responsibilities that the Freemen of "DEER SOUND" carried out their very

132

difficult and onerous duties in initiating some 500 Novices in the Mysteries of the Sea.

To the great gratification of the Freemen the following signal from His Majesty was received at 0900 on 6th February:—

To: The Commanding Officer,

His Britannic Majesty's Ship of War

"DEER SOUND."

From: The Equator W/T Station.

It is reported by my amphibian scouts that H.M.S. "DEER SOUND" intends to enter His Maritime Majesty King Neptune's domain. Please confirm this, in order that my chamberlains may prepare to receive you. His Maritime Majesty The King commands that all his loyal subjects in

"DEER SOUND" will take the necessary steps to receive him. Our bears are plentiful and hungry.

Clerk of the Rolls.

The following reply was immediately sent:

Please convey to their Majesties humble duty of all friends on board. "DEER SOUND" expects to enter Royal domain on sixth day of February. Bear food rich and plentiful.

9999 Johnson.

Later that day, equatorial seagulls hovering overhead dropped the following on the Officer of the Watch (the bridge awning stations having collapsed):

Whereas we have been informed of the projected visit of His Majesty's Ship "DEER SOUND" to our domain, and whereas, after diligent search, the superscriptions of divers members of the crew of that ship have not been found within our archives. You are hereby summoned to furnish me, upon arrival in our domain, with a full and complete list of the aforesaid superscriptions in order that we may confer upon them the "Freedom of the Seas" and our permission to enter the other hemisphere.

Dated this forty-fourth day of Octopus, at the hour of 0000 F.F.T. (Flying Fish Time) 774945 Anno Piscis.

(Signed) Barnacle Bill,

Lord Chief Justice.

at the hour of 0930 on the 7th day of February, One Thousand Nine Hundred and Forty-five.

By these Presents we summon you to appear at the said court to tender us the usual homage, and to be initiated into the mystic rites according to the ancient usages of our Kingdom.

Herefore nor you, nor any of you may fail, as you will answer at your peril and to the delight of our trusty bodyguard.

Given at our Court on the Equator this 6th day of February in the year One Thousand Nine Hundred and Forty-five of our Watery Reign.

NEPTUNUS REX MARIS.

Great consternation was caused in the Master-At-Arms mess when a Flying Fish touched down bearing the following:

A SUMMONS TO ALL LANDLUBBERS

45th Day of Octopus,

0001 F.F.T. (Flying Fish Time)

774945 Anno Piscis.

Neptune, by Grace of Mythology, Lord of all the Waters, Sovereign of all the Oceans, Governor and Lord High Admiral of the Bath etc., etc., etc.

Whereas it has pleased us to convene a court to be holden on board His Britannic Majesty's Ship "DEER SOUND" on the after well deck thereof.

And orders of investiture which he was charged to deliver (specimen below):

NOTICE OF INVESTITURE

WHEREAS by your good sea records and honourable calling you are hereby summoned to attend the Ancient and Honourable Ceremony of Investiture that will raise you to the high degree of ORDER OF CRAMPUS.

The holding of such Royal and Ancient Charter will render you inviolate from attacks of Swordfish, Walrus and Barracuda, so even adamant against the more deadly and potent wiles of Mermaids, Nymphs or other alluring immortals.

Be it known to all mortals you are possessed of this degree.

The greatest honour conferred upon a follower of the Sea.

DAVY JONES,   NEPTUNE.

Clerk of the Rolls,   Rex Maris.

The summons, having been perused by the Captain, was then placed in the Recreation Space, afterwards being exhibited in the Wardroom to the noticeable discomfiture of certain landlubbers in our midst. The Line was actually crossed at 0400 in longitude . . . (censored), but, being pitch dark at the time, it was quite invisible. His Majesty, accompanied by Queen Amphitrite and the Court having the comfort and well-being of his subjects always at heart, boarded "DEER SOUND" at 0930 on the 7th February, 1945, and, fortified by a hearty breakfast addressed the Captain thus:

NEPTUNE:

"Ship ahoy! What ship—at least it ship it be.
What strange projections o'er the side I see?
Can it be you are now on pleasure bound?
This lack of guns to me seems damned unsound.
Ship ahoy! What ship—where from and whither for?
Ye are now in my domain and far from Britain's shore.
Captain, you have candidates who cannot leave the lead;
Do not know the Deep Sea lore or how a Mermaid's fed."

CAPTAIN:

"His Britannic Majesty's Ship "DEER SOUND"
From Colombo to Sydney."

NEPTUNE:

"Avast there! a strange ship I see,
It's quite a brand new class to me.
I think that from its rotund line
It may have pops at almost any time,
Her Captain I have met before,
Some years ago, I think, a scene.
He then appeared before me as a callow boy,
To see him with four rings gives me pride and joy.
My Court and Bears will now proceed and carry
    through
The initiation of all and sundry of your crew,
Of those who go down to the sea in ships,
Not the novice who takes short sea trips,
So that, when duly initiated in the mystery as seamen,
They may become our loyal, great and worthy
    Freemen.
The homage that to me is my just due
Must be paid by all except the few,
To those to whom this honour is conferred
I give the bond of Neptune and my word.

CAPTAIN:

"Your Majesty's distinguished speech
Has charmed the ears of all and each.
So while, not wishing to complain

Of anything in your domain
Or spoiling the Atlantic's jest
By asking for a moment's rest.
A lot of us would like to see
How really flat the sea can be.
So earn our lasting gratitude
By smoothing the South Latitude.
And now, sir, pray proceed aright
My compliments to Amphitrite."

NEPTUNE:

"Very Good, Very Good."

Neptune now received a statement from the Clerk of Rolls showing list of Freemen and Landlubbers. The Clerk of Rolls addressed the Captain thus:

Keeper of the Purse and Slave.
Chief Bear and Official Taster.
Neptune and Amphitrite (in chariot drawn by 8 bears).
Ladies in Waiting.
Lord Chief Justice and Lord Chamberlain.
Clerk of Rolls and Assistant Clerk of Rolls.
Court Physicians.
Barbers.

The magnificent Royal Chariots were halted and greeted by a fanfare of trumpets. Their Majesties mounted the tastefully decorated dais and were duly enthroned.

"By inspection of the records of your crew
I find there are some several hundreds who
Have never earned the Freedom of the Sea,
A most distressing state you must agree.
Reports have reached us that the slightest swell
Have caused these landlubbers to feel unwell.
Such ill behaviour we shall shortly try
And do our very best to rectify."

The Captain and all available hands assembled on the afterwell deck, which had been suitably prepared for His Majesty's reception, and the full Court with all its pomp and dignity moved aft in procession in the following order:

Heralds (bearing orders).
Chief of Police and Policemen.

(A description of the structure on which the proceedings of the Court were carried out will not be out of place here. On the right was the Operating Table in charge of the Court Physicians, suitably attired and prepared to carry out any major operation —a supply of pills, spare hearts, ribs, etc., being readily at hand. At the rear was Their Majesties seated on two simple but regal thrones. Their personal retinue was in attendance including, in addition to the Maids of Honour, the Keeper of the Purse and his Slave. The Maids of Honour with their golden curls and fresh complexions were typical of the innocent beauty of His Majesty's domain. The right of the dais was occupied by the Clerk of the Rolls and his Assistant, all in their appropriate robes. Order

The Official Taster took his seat and was lathered, shaved and tipped into the bath, to be courteously received by the Bears, who saw to it that he had plenty of opportunity to taste the waters.

When at last he broke surface he addressed the Royal Personage: "Your Majesty's orders have been obeyed. I have tasted the Waters."

NEPTUNE: "And what do you find?"

OFFICIAL TASTER: "I find them as they should be."

NEPTUNE: "Then I declare this Court open, and let the ceremony commence."

The initiation opened with a warrant being issued against Captain R. H. Johnson, D.S.C., R.N., which was read by the Lord Chamberlain in the following words:—

YOU ARE BROUGHT BEFORE THIS COURT AND CHARGED WITH IN-DECENT HASTE, THEREBY DEPRIVING LOYAL SUBJECTS OF THE FRUITS OF THEIR LIQUORS, THAT IS, ENJOYING THE PLEASURE OF AMOROUS MER-MAIDS; ALSO WHILE RISING TO YOUR EXALTED POSITION FAILING TO VISIT US."

DAVY JONES,   NEPTUNE,
Clerk of the Rolls.   Rex Maris.

The Lord Chief Justice pronounced the following punishment:—Two pills, hair-cut and shave and to be ducked twice, this being considered by all a very light sentence for such peculiar behaviour. The Court Photographer, during the carrying out of the sentence, took numerous photographs as a permanent record of the just punishment meted out to this malefactor.

Facing the Royal Personages, but at a discreet distance away at the edge of the platform, the novices were in turn placed on two pivoted chairs. Here the Court Barbers lathered and shaved their victims before tilting the unsuspecting novices into the bath for the fondling caresses of the awaiting Bears. The speed and efficiency of this proceeding was most commendable. Sometimes resistance was offered, but the well organised police were always at hand to proffer their assistance, and needless to say the unruly novice led

the severe punishment that was immediately administered.

On mounting the platform, the novices first passed the Court Scribes, who registered their names. Next they were entrusted to the Court Physicians to test their fitness to undergo the somewhat strenuous ordeal before them. Elaborate thermometers of a most sensitive order were in use, and with the careful administration of pills, the novices—if still surviving—were handed over to the Barbers. Seated in the chairs, a lather of delightful messes followed by a shave with a magnificent Court Razor demanded the novice's full attention, after which, the very unsuspecting beings were, without warning tipped over backwards to suffer the tender embraces of the hungry bears.

On his arrival on board and subsequently at frequent intervals His Majesty expressed his pleasure and delight at meeting once again that small but select band of freemen in "DEER SOUND." It was obvious, however, that His Majesty was displeased and somewhat suspicious at his Consort's scintillating eyes and the coy winsome glances she bestowed on both Freemen and Novices alike. This may have led to the remarks passed by some Rabelaisian-minded individual, who said—"Amphitrite, she should be called Anthracite, she looks hot stuff to me."

This comment was duly traced by the Royal Sleuth Hounds, and heavily punished.

Here a word to the skill and proficiency of the

remaining novices' chagrin and consternation it was noticed that a number of lean and hungry bears had appeared, some of their predecessors having become slothful and lethargic through over-indulgence. Resistance of a sustained character was offered by various novices, but the efficiency and long experience of the Deep Sea Police in dealing with malcontents was equal to each and every occasion. In a few cases the strait-jacket was necessary to coax the victim to the top of the platform. The Chief of Police and his Force was highly commended by His Majesty for executing his orders so proficiently.

A deep growl came from the bears and His Majesty rose in wrath when one offender was charged

Court Physicians be mentioned, as, throughout the whole proceedings, only one tiny untoward incident occurred; this being when an offender was almost decapitated. Since "Up Spirits" had been sounded this near miss was readily understandable.

At eleven thirty, Queen Amphitrite was heard to remark, in clear bell-like tones, that she was choked with watching novices imbibe quantities of salt water, so how about His Majesty escorting her to the Bar. His Majesty announced that he was entirely in agreement, and also wished to set tooth to garbage (as provided by Commander (S). He thereupon adjourned the court until 1330.

The Court duly re-assembled and much to the re-

that he did, among other heinous offences, refer to our Solemn Court as "entertainment," and to the heavy sentences pronounced by the Lord Chief Justice His Majesty ordered the culprit to have his brains removed and a more suitable set inserted. It was observed that large quantities of blood were shed during this delicate operation, and to the stupefaction of the Court Physicians, the criminal surfaced with ultramarine-coloured ears, a most unlooked for result.

Another unspeakable scoundrel of the gigolo type was charged with casting licentious glances at Amphitrite. His Majesty immediately demanded certain measures, and it was only after remonstrations from the Queen that the Judge tempered justice with mercy.

A very long list of novices still remained to be dealt with and no time was lost in appeasing His Maritime Majesty's righteous anger at the presence of so many —never before has so much been done to so many by so few. It was with a sigh of relief from the Bears that the Clerk of Rolls reported, "Your Majesty, no novices remain."

His Majesty then expressed a desire to taste the waters personally, and having been ceremoniously lathered and shaved by his own personal barbers, shot into the Bath as though jet-propelled, and clasping Amphitrite to his bosom disappeared beneath the surface of the waters, followed by his whole court.

To end a perfect day, the only known recording of His Majesty's voice broadcast over the S.R.E. in which King Neptune bade adieu to his new subjects in "DEER SOUND" in the following words:—

"Hark: all ye infants enrolled as my Freemen,
Before I return to my wreck-covered shores,
See you stand by the kinship of all worthy seamen,
And hold fast to the faith of the sea and its laws."

The following messages were received that night and bear testimony to Their Majesties' visit, and to our having crossed the Line in Longitude . . . . (Censored).

FROM:—Equatorial Headquarters.
"On behalf of Queen Amphitrite, Myself and Court, I desire to thank you, Captain Johnson Royal Navy, for the general facilities you gave us, and the detailed efforts made on our behalf to make our visit such a memorably happy and enjoyable one.

"I also congratulate you on being in command of such a very fine ship, manned by an equally fine crew."

FROM:—Equatorial Headquarters.
"In connection with my visit on the 7th February, 1945, I desire on behalf of Queen Amphitrite, myself and the Court, to thank the Officers and Ship's Company of His Britannic Majesty's ship "DEER SOUND" for being such perfect hosts, and in turn becoming equally charming and sportsmanlike guests during the initiation ceremony, when over 500 of their long shoremen were made Noble and Worthy Sons of the Sea."

DRAMATIS PERSONAE.

NEPTUNE: Cdr. Roser.
AMPHITRITE: S/L.(S) Moody
MAIDS OF HONOUR: C.P.O. McCarthy,
 A.B. Bamber
LORD CHAMBERLAIN: Lt. Andrew
LORD CHIEF JUSTICE: C.P.O. Knight
CLERK OF THE ROLLS: Lt.(S) Millard
ASSISTANT CLERK OF THE ROLLS:
 A.B. Levy

KEEPER OF THE PURSE: Cdr.(S)
 Hawley
SLAVE: A.B. Grant
OFFICIAL TASTER: Mr. Watts, W.S.O.
CHIEF OF POLICE: Lt. Newell
CHIEF BEAR: Mr. Martin, Wt. Engr.
HERALDS: S.C.P.O. Daffey, P.O. Murdock
COURT PHOTOGRAPHER: S/Lt.(A)
 Puller

COURT PHYSICIANS:

Lt. (A) Mayer	Lt. Ford
Mr. Papworth, Gar.	Lt. East

BARBERS:

Mr. Forrest, W.A.O.	P.O. Quinn
Ck. Farrow	S.C.P.O. Smeeta
C.E.A. Connolly	St. P.O. Darvill
Lt. Cdr.(E) Scott	P.O. Whitehead

BEARS:

S/Lt. Alwyn-Smith	S/L. MacDonald
A.B. Fowkes	A.B. Hayes
St. P.O. Spriddle	O.A. Bayliss
S.A. Moule	Std. Tweedale
Sail. Howard	A.B. Bater
C.P.O. Rice	Sto. Havetina
P.O. Allpert	P.O. Miller
Sail. Hodgson	A.A. Roberts

POLICE:

P.O. Margerrison	R.P.O. Brown
P.O. Dodd	P.O. Hall
A.B. Jameson	P.O. Miller
Skpt. Hevenn	L.S.A. McGahey
L.S. Kilgore	L.S. Bauley
L. Ck. Douglas	P.O.Ok. Henton
L.Sig. Bray	L.S. Colman
P.O. Evans	A.B. Mills

AWARDS:

ORDER OF SEA DOG: Captain R. H. Johnson, D.S.C., R.N.

ORDER OF ST. FUMIGATOR WITH SWORDS: Lieutenant East, R.N.R.

ORDER OF ZIG-ZAG GUIDING LIGHT: Lieutenant Ford, R.N.R.

ORDER OF FLYING FISH: Lieutenant Mayer, R.N.V.R.

ORDER OF PINK PANTIES: Lieutenant Newell, R.C.N.V.R.

ORDER OF THE TWISTED WHEEL: Petty Officer Margerrison.

ORDER OF THE MERMAID WITH CRABS: Petty Officer Ryan.

ORDER OF MAIN THRUST BLOCK: Lieutenant-Commander Scott, R.N.

ORDER OF MERIT WITH CROSSED
RIBS: Mr. Forrest, Warrant Air Officer, R.N.

ORDER OF GRAMPUS: Mr. Watts, Warrant Stores Officer, R.N.

ORDER OF DEHYDRATED SEAWEED:
Commander Hawley, R.N.R.

MEDAL OF SHELLBACK, FIRST CLASS:
Leading Seaman Bailey
Stoker Haveron
Regulating Petty Officer Brown
Chief Petty Officer Knight
Able Seaman Love
Chief Petty Officer McCarthy

Mr. Papworth, Gunner, R.N.

Able Seaman Bamber

Chief Petty Officer Connolly

Chief Petty Officer Rice

Mr. Martin, Warrant Engineer, R.N.

Able Seaman Grant

Chief Petty Officer Duffey

Lieutenant Andrew, R.N.R.

Lieutenant Millard, R.N.V.R.

Sub-Lieutenant Alwyn-Smith, R.N.V.R.

Sub-Lieutenant MacDonald, R.N.V.R.

Sailmaker Hodgson

Petty Officer Henton

SELECTION OF WARRANTS:

COMMANDER—

YOU ARE BROUGHT BEFORE THIS
COURT AND CHARGED THAT YOU DID
SLIGHT OURSELVES AND THIS MOST
HONOURABLE COURT BY

(1) HAVING THE EFFRONTERY TO
BOARD HIS BRITANNIC
MAJESTY'S SHIP "DEER SOUND"
WEARING A "BRASS HAT" AND
ASSUMING COMMAND OF SOME
400 LANDLUBBERS WITHOUT

(2) EVER HAVING BEEN TO SEA, OR

(3) ENTERED HIS MARITIME
MAJESTY'S DOMAIN

(4) WEARING THREE STRIPES WITH-
OUT SCRAMBLED EGGS.

LIEUTENANT—

YOU ARE BROUGHT BEFORE THIS
COURT AND CHARGED WITH OGLING
MERMAIDENS AND CASTING LICEN-
TIOUS GLANCES AT AMPHITRITE.

SUB-LIEUTENANT—

IS BROUGHT BEFORE THIS COURT
AND CHARGED WITH, LESE MAJESTY,
HERESY AND HIGH TREASON IN THAT
HE DID REFER TO THIS COURT AND
THESE SOLEMN PROCEEDINGS AS
ENTERTAINMENT.

SUB-LIEUTENANT—

IS BROUGHT BEFORE THIS COURT AND CHARGED THAT HE DID ALLOW A FUNGUS TO BECOME APPARENT ON HIS LOWER JAW, THEREBY LIBELLING THE USE OF SPUNYARD.

CHIEF PETTY OFFICER—

IS BROUGHT BEFORE THIS COURT AND CHARGED WITH HAVING WOE-FULLY AND DELIBERATELY EN-DEAVOURED TO D E C E I V E BOTH NOVICES AND FREEMEN BY ASSUMING THE GUISE OF AN ANCIENT SEA DOG IN APPEARING IN MY DOMAIN FOR THE FIRST TIME WITH THREE BUT-TONS, SCANT OF HAIR ON HEAD, AND UNYOUTHFUL OF GIRTH AND GAIT, THEREBY BELYING HIS TENDER YEARS.

DID ALSO S H O C K AND PRO-FOUNDLY DISTURB MANY OF MY MOST TRUSTED FREEMEN BY REFERRING TO SCUTTLES AS "WINDOWS" AND LADDERS AS "STAIRS."

CANTEEN MANAGER—

IS BROUGHT BEFORE THIS COURT AND CHARGED WITH

(1) ROBBERY WITH VIOLENCE

(2) DISTURBING THE REST OF MER-MAIDS BY ATROCIOUS PLAYING OF PIANO.

HMS PERSEUS

The following booklet is supplied by the Royal Navy Research Archives, courtesy of Eddie Wright, former Air Mechanic (Airframes).

November 1945, HMS PERSEUS in the Suez Canal on her way out to Join the BPF. Photo courtesy Maurice Ayling.

The members of mess 20 HMS Perseus pose in front of an aircraft lighter. Eddie Wright is middle row first from right.

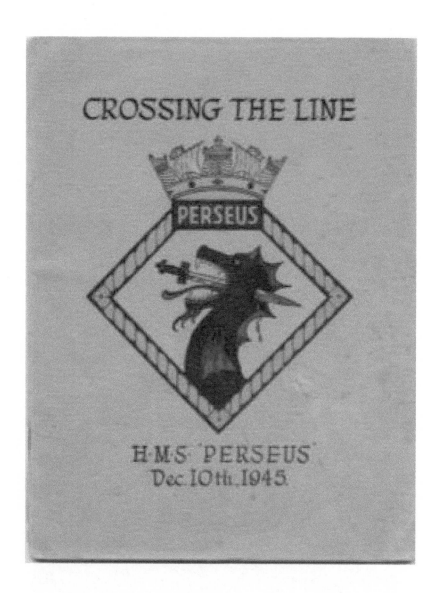

"Crossing the Line"

CEREMONY

HELD ON BOARD

H.M.S. "PERSEUS"

CAPTAIN G. R. DEVERELL, R.N.

Ship on Passage from

Southampton to Sydney, Australia

December 10th, 1945

The Court and Officials

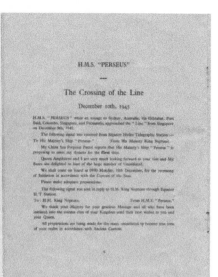

H.M.S. "PERSEUS"

The Crossing of the Line

December 10th, 1945

Arrival of King Neptune's Ambassador

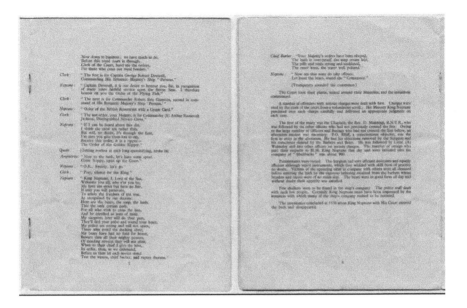

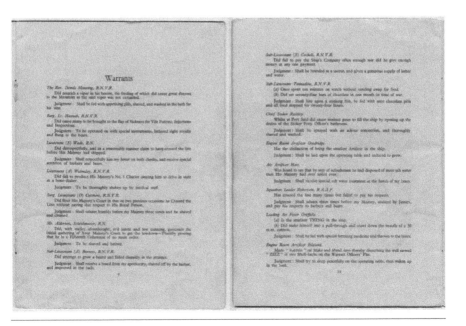

Regulating Petty Officer Cane.
Did accuse the Clerk of the Court of not Crossing the Line.

Judgment : Shall salaam three times to my Clerk of the Court, and lathered down to the line, then receive water treatment.

Petty Officer (S) O'Neill.
Did pipe a Stop Issue in the Dog Watches thereby taking away good Sailors' Recreational time.

Judgment : Shall be shown a new form of Physical Diatribe by our alchemist.

Petty Officer Elliff.
Did make a false statement to wit, that he had entered His Majesty's Domain on a previous occasion thereby trying to dodge the column.

Judgment : Shall swear never to tell another lie, persuaded by surgical instruments and held on high by my bears.

Able Seaman Wyatt.
Did pipe " Special Sea Dutymen " in the middle of the Indian Ocean, thereby raising the hopes of his messmates for a run ashore.

Judgment : Shall be treated by my doctor and thrown to the bears.

Able Seaman Ward.
Did cause concern and wonderment among the ship's company by piping "Hands to shift into make and mend clothes."

Judgment : Shall be sawn into several pieces, and thrown to the bears.

The Canteen Manager.
Did endeavour to delay the entry of the ship into the Royal Domain by producing 10,000 bags of pickled walnuts at the gangway five minutes before sailing.

Judgment : Shall be liberally slapped by a big fish, specially dieted, the scales removed by barbers and bears.

Able Seaman King.
Showed ignorance in the pastime of the Ocean by asking " What's this game of Tombola ?"

Judgment : Shall be taught to say " full house " and " line " to the satisfaction of my Jester and receive his winnings in the bath.

Air Mechanic Iles.
During a flat calm, the sea just breaking over the bridge, was stricken with a strange malady called sea-sickness.

Judgment : Shall make a vomiting noise, receive eyes out sickness medicine, and retire to salt water.

11

Writer Elliff.
Did fall on any and every occasion to type a true copy of the original draft.

Judgment : Shall chant out loudly " I am dreaming of my darling love of Bliss," to the satisfaction of my Queen.

Air Mechanic Gardner.
Did say at dinner time " Don't bother about the vals—let me breathe on your scran."

Judgment : Shall receive a special mouth treatment, lathered from top to bottom by the barbers and stimulated by the bears.

Petty Officer Horn.
Did intimate that he was the son of one " Tyador Horn " who had crossed the line more times than His Majesty had hot dinners.

Judgment : Shall receive hot dinner treatment, the soles of his feet toasted and cooled off in the bath.

Air Artificer Leitch.
Did claim that he crossed the line with full ceremony in 1922 in a Spitfire, a statement of doubtful veracity.

Judgment : Shall be lifted on high, make a noise like a Spitfire, and thrown to the bears.

Leading Air Fitter Smith.
Being an ex-apprentice did try to make his messmates believe he was group 44 by wearing his cap flat-a-back and gorgeorines.

Judgment : You shall be branded with your true group number shaved back and fresh, and make space for the bears.

Shipwright (S) Bartlett.
Did show disrespect to His Majesty in that he did fail to appreciate the honour of entering His Majesty's Domain and did break his vows of Melancholy by smiling at least once and causing them to hit messmates.

Judgment : Shall be tickled on the soles of your feet until you laugh loudly, and pursue your melancholy way through the bath.

Petty Officer Martin.
Did write the name of the ship with its suite when passing through His Majesty's Ocean but failed to prefix it with " H.M.S.", thereby causing confusion to His Majesty as to whether the ship was a Warship, Steamship, Hardship or the Gosport Ferry.

Judgment : Shall be taught to steer a steady course, dosed with anti-drunk mixture, and write his name in the bath.

12

SS WARRIMOO

The Strange Story of the SS Warrimoo.

This story is much repeated as an absolute fact, but I can only entertain it as an anecdotal account because I have not been able to locate any proven or undisputed documented evidence.

I am including it here primarily for its curiosity and entertainment value.

Captain J (John) D. S. Phillips was Master of the 3326-ton S.S. Warrimoo, (*sometimes referred to as the RMS Warrimoo*), of the Canadian – Australian Lines in 1899 and 1900.

He is listed as Master when the (Sydney) Evening News of October 17th, 1900 reported SS Warrimoo as arriving Sydney on October 16th, 1900 from Vancouver via Honolulu and Brisbane with 32 passengers on board.

It is said the Warrimoo 'Crossed the Line' on New Year's Eve 1899, during this voyage, whilst sailing across the Pacific Ocean.

The story continues saying the navigator finished working out a star fix and brought the results to Captain Phillips immediately.

Captain Phillips took full advantage to achieve a navigational freak of a lifetime.

He called his navigator to the bridge to check and double check the ship's position. The Warrimoo's position was latitude 0 degrees x 31 minutes north and longitude 179 degrees x 30 minutes west.

The Captain ordered a change, of course, to bear directly on his navigator's mark. He then he adjusted the engine speed.

The calm weather and clear night worked in his favour.

At midnight precisely the Warrimoo lay on the Equator at exactly the point where it crossed the International Date Line, *(as depicted in the accompanying image.)*

The consequences of Captain Phillips's diversion of course and speed were many.

On the precise stroke of midnight, when the Warrimoo was Crossing the Line, the forward part of the ship was in the Southern Hemisphere in the middle of summer. The stern was in the Northern Hemisphere in the middle of winter.

The date in the aft part of the ship was 31 December 1899, while forward it was 1 January 1900.

This ship was positioned such, it not only in the two different hemispheres, but it was also in two different days, two different months, two different seasons and two different years.

Even more so, it was in two different centuries, all at the same time.*28

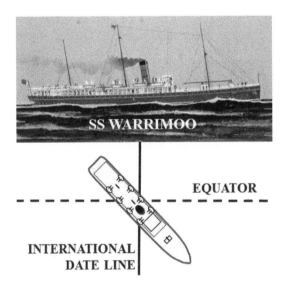

---

28 Ref; (A), Passenger Ships of Australia and New Zealand.

(B), Crossed Flags, (World Ship Society).

Exactly one century later, there was an opportunity for a commemorative voyage; but sadly, not aboard the SS Warrimoo.

In late 1914, during the first world war, the Warrimoo was taken up as a troopship, delivering the first Maori Pioneer military troops to Gallipoli in 1915.

On 17 May 1918 when on a convoy from Bizerta to Marseille she collided with the escorting French destroyer 'Catapulte'.

Catapulte's depth-charges were dislodged, exploded in the water and blowing out the bottom plates of both ships, causing both to sink with several losses of life.

SS Warrimoo	
Bow	**Stern**
Southern	Northern
Summer	Winter
Midnight	**Midnight**
Monday	Sunday
1st	31st
January	December
1900	1899
20th	19th

Author's note:

I did say I only accept this yarn as an anecdotal dit, even if it is one which mixes fact and fiction together wonderfully.

Now, before any anal-retentive seamen mention this fact, the years 1899 and 1900 are both parts of the 19th century. The 20th century did not 'technically' begin until 1st of January 1901.

Moreover, for the scientifically-minded, sextants read the angle between the sun, or another star and the horizon.

If you can get this measurement down to an accuracy of a 60th of a degree, or 1 minute, there is a leeway of 1 nautical mile in your calculated position. With a very good sextant and excellent procedure, that window narrows to .2 of a minute. That's 1/5th of a mile.

However, the operative word here is 'if', as this is an accuracy many navigators long to achieve.

To calculate longitude, one also needs a highly accurate timepiece. Being off by one second of time puts your position off by 1/4 of a mile.

Most ships of this period carried several clocks and generally the time was averaged using three or four of them, another critical point for an error to occur.

So, given all that, it's unlikely the SS Warrimoo nailed its position accurately at exactly the right moment.

However, it is wonderful to consider the possibility.

ACKNOWLEDGEMENTS

Andrew Alderson, one of my old shipmates, for supplying his father's photographs. One which I selected for the cover image.

Tony Drury, of Royal Navy Research Archives, for research documentation, photographs and for pestering me to compile this book.

Another old shipper, *R Rodgers* (Bob), for allowing me to reproduce his own Crossing the line certificate from HMS Tiger, in 1973.

The National Maritime Museum, Greenwich, London. For information on HMS Rifleman.

The National Library of Australia, for checking on copyright status regarding HMS Deer Sound.

Henry Stommel, for founding the internet archive in 1996 and creating a wealth of research material on just about every subject imaginable. I am happy to be a donator and supporter of this amazing resource. https://archive.org

Eddie Wright, Air Mechanic (Airframes), HMS Perseus, 1945.

ABOUT THE AUTHOR

Paul White was born in Portsmouth, the traditional home of the Royal Navy, which he joined a few months prior to his sixteenth birthday.

After his naval career, he found himself 'slowly drifting northwards', until he arrived in the East Riding of Yorkshire and fell for a 'Northern lass'.

"I have now lived here for over thirty years," he says, *"in another thirty, I expect I shall no longer be classed as a newcomer."*

Paul writes from his home, situated near a quiet market town in the East Ridings. He is a prolific storyteller, a wordsmith, tale weaver and an international bestselling author.

Paul has published several books, from full-length novels to short story collections, poetry, children's books, semi-fiction and, of course, his books which focus on Royal Naval social history.

He says, *"I think recording the social aspect of Royal Naval life is extremely important. It is an area most academics overlook but one which is rich in knowledge and, of course, the human element."*

He continues, *"It is only now the home records, the personal diaries, family photographs and the odd surviving reel of private cinematic film from the past, such as the first Great War, are being realised as some of the most valuable historical information.*

With Neptune and the Pollywogs, along with my other books regarding the Royal Navy, I hope to capture the same illusive personal and social elements as a testimony to a way of life which is too quickly becoming lost in the passing sea mists of time as progress marches inexorably onwards."

You can find more about Paul, his current works-in-progress, artworks and other projects, by visiting his website:

http://paulznewpostbox.wix.com/paul-white

OTHER BOOKS BY PAUL WHITE

FICTION

The Abduction of Rupert DeVille

(A Novel - Paperback & eBook)

Tales of Crime & Violence

(Short story collections - Volumes 1, 2 & 3)

Dark Words

Dark Tales – Darker poetry

(Short stories & poetry combined - Paperback)

SEMI-FICTION

Life in the War Zone

(True life stories from areas of conflict - Paperback)

POETRY

Teardrops & White Doves

(Paperback, eBook & Outsized Hardcover)

Shadows of Emotion

(Paperback & eBook)

MILITARY SOCIAL HISTORY

HMS Tiger -Chronicles of the last big cat

(Outsized Hardcover only)

The Pussers Cook Book

(Paperback & Hardcover)

Jack's Dits – Tall Tales from the Mess

(Paperback)

CHILDREN'S STORIES

The Rabbit Joke

(A 'read to me' book - Outsized Hardcover)

A Treasure chest of children's stories

(Anthology)

MUSIC/ART

Iconic

(Collectors limited edition - Hardcover only)

ANTHOLOGIES

(Joint Author/contributor)

Awethors anthology – *Light volume*

Awethors December anthology – *Dark volume*

Individually Together

(Storybook publishing)

Looking into the Abyss

(TOAD Publishing)

A Treasure chest of children's stories

(Plaisted publishing house)

Midsummer Anthology

(Jara publishing)

ELECTRIC ECLECTIC BOOKS

(ebook/Amazon)

Miriam's Hex (black humour/urban fiction)

Three Floors Up (psychological suspense)

Mechanical Mike (Pulp fiction/comic book sci-fi)

A New Summer Garden (Crime fiction)

North to Maynard (Urban/ghost in the machine)

The Amulet (Ancient magic meets modern day)

The Orb (Fast paced action chase)